FROM
THE
ROCKING
CHAIR

A catalogue record for this book is available from the National Library of Australia at catalogue.nla.gov.au

Cover and internal design and layout by Tess McCabe
www.tessmccabe.com.au

Edited by Rebecca Tisdale

Paperback ISBN 978-0-6453305-0-2
Ebook ISBN 978-0-6453305-1-9

Printed in Australia / worldwide by Ingram Spark

Instagram @fromtherockingchair

DISCLAIMER
The views, opinions and thoughts expressed in this book belong solely to the author and are intended for the purpose of entertainment. This book should not be used as a substitute for professional assistance, therapeutic support or medical advice. In the event of physical or mental distress, please consult with appropriate health professionals. The application of ideas and information presented in this book are the choice of the reader, who assumes full responsibility for their understanding, interpretation or results. The author assumes no responsibility for the actions or choices of any reader.

FROM THE ROCKING CHAIR

a collection of motherhood
poetry and prose

JESSICA DRISCOLL

To my daughter, H

My greatest inspiration.

I will spend forever trying to find the words
to show you just how much I love you.

CONTENTS

From the rocking chair   5

one
MY LOVE FOR YOU

Love you like no other   8
Soft   9
Dream come true   10
Being held by your child   11
Lemon drops   12
The pull   13
Bedtime   14
Home and haven   16
You and I   17
My child, my own   18
Love you for you   19

two
IN MY ARMS, IN MY HEART

Of course it is you   22
Baby button nose   23
This body   24
Curled into me   26
Favourite time of day   27
Footsteps beneath the moon   28

Bedtime   29
Here   30
I love you I love you I love you   31
Contact nap   32
Rest upon me   33
Look at you   34
Holiday season   36
When a child needs their mother   37
The days of little you   38
Gentle wave to the day   39

three
MOTHERING

Mother   42
The way of a mother   43
The beauty in the imperfection   44
The flame   45
I am but 'Mother'   46
Motherhood CV   48
Coming over   50
Need to leave the house   52
Sticky floors   54
This tiredness   55
The mother, the moor   56
The slowing   57

The mental load   58
Energy   60
So tired   62
Exhaustion   64
Just   66
To mother   67
Had to leave you   68
Wasn't it just the beginning?   70
Taking care   71

four
OLD FRIENDS, NEW
FRIENDS, PLEASE BEAR
WITH ME DEAR FRIENDS
Before I was a mum   74
Little conversations   76
Little note   77
Bear with me   78
Conversations   80
Mum friends   82

five
MOTHER, ME
The birth of you   86
The time we need to heal   88
Mother's strength   90
Everyday magic   91
Stronger   92
All of me   93
Simply as I am   94
INSOMNIA!   96
Breathe at last   97
Overwhelm   98

Whole again   99
If I met her now   100
Selfies   102
Time with me   104
I am mother   105

six
IN THE NIGHT
Effortless   108
Rest your head with me love   109
4am   110
Broken lines   111
Hand to chest   112
Mummy   113
In the midst of slumber   114
Big king bed   115
I love it in the night-time   116
Butterflies of slumber   117
Always be your home   118

seven
MILKY BREATH
Milky breath   122
Sunshine   123
How long?   124
Latched in slumber   126
Out and about   127
Side to side   128
Little mouth   129
Mastitis   130
Pumping   131
Little acrobat   132
I grew for you   133

eight
OTHER LOVE
One day you will know   136
The centre of it all   137
When I hug my mother   138
Us   140
Her grandmother, her friend   142
The one that we call home   143
Need you   144
Oh, my heart   145
To my own mother   146
My dear friend, the mother   147
Travel time   148
My husband, your daddy   150
Father   151

nine
INTUITION
All I heard was you   154
I'm right here   156
Feed to sleep   158
Vulnerability   159
Crying   160
Clung to me   161
Human   162
Brave   163
Say no   164
Childhood   165
The comfort   166
Move to you   167
Lost herself   168
Today   170

A need all of its own   171
The books say   172
Surrender   173

ten
WATCHING YOU GROW
Slow down, time   176
The ocean   177
In the dark   178
I want you to know   179
Before you grow a little more   180
On the run   182
Smiles   184
In wonder   186
Playing on your own   188
This bed   190
Puddles   191
Rush through life   192
Tweet tweet   194
The little things   196
Laughing in your sleep   198
Watch you grow   199

Acknowledgements   201
About the author   202

FROM THE ROCKING CHAIR

With the to and fro of the rocking chair
The words began to spin

Prose, they flowed, and couplets turned
To poems from within

The depths of this new mother's mind
Consumed in its new phase

The discovery of my truest self
In my daughter's early days.

And, with that, a book was born
The one that you read now

The story of my motherhood
And the phases all throughout.

From early days to toddlerhood
This is my greatest try

To put in words my love for her
And this tale of her and I.

one

MY LOVE FOR YOU

LOVE YOU
LIKE NO
OTHER

"My baby" I say to myself
Letting the words fall softly out

In disbelief, you are here with me
The one I dreamed about.

Darling child, don't you know
I love you like no other

That before you came into this world
No one had called me mother.

And when it was you came to be
So, in a way, did I

The moment you lay on my chest
And gazed into my eyes.

I pull you close, breathe you in
Soak in your sweet face

Hold you in this rocking chair
Our most beloved place

And whisper 'Darling, don't you know
I love you like no other?

For you made me who I am today,
The one that you call "mother"'.

SOFT

This tiny hand
The softest skin

The gentleness of you
That I grew within

Is the cure and the care
The mender of all

The suspender of time
The rise from the fall.

No matter the cause
The resolve is the same

The elixir of joy
Embodied, and named.

The essence of you
Just you as you are

With one touch of your hand
You heal my heart.

DREAM
COME
TRUE

It astounds me

the magnificent simplicity of this life with you.

How your little smile can scatter even the darkest of skies with the light of a million stars.

Some moments I find myself captivated by you

lost in thoughts of the you I had dreamt of

wondering, always, who you would be

who you would look like, sound like

who... who?... who?

Now I see

it is you.

I exhale into you

the existence and reality of you, my sweet child

Realising that not only are you everything I had dreamt of

but more.

So much more.

Magnificently, simply

You.

BEING HELD BY YOUR CHILD

Is there any feeling quite like
When the arms of your child

Reach for you, requesting to
Embrace a little while?

My darling, when you hold me
My worries fall away

I forget about the housework
And the stresses of the day.

My darling, when you hold me
It becomes so very clear

I thought that it was only you
That needed me near.

But I see it now, darling
Clearer every day

That it is I that needs you too
That this need, it goes both ways.

I feel it when I hold you
That sighing of my soul

The comfort and relief as I'm
Made, once again, whole.

Yes, you need me darling
I knew that from the start

But I know now that I need you too
With all my mother heart.

LEMON DROPS

Your laughter falls like lemon drops
Upon my mother ear

Signs of your sweet happiness
The sweetest thing to hear.

For darling, don't you know it?
That part within my soul

That sat so bare before you?
Well now, with you, it's whole.

Your smile brightens darkness
No other light can find

Brilliant diamonds sparkling
That ease the mother mind.

For darling, don't you know it?
That portion of my heart

That sat in ache and want for you
And wished on every star?

Your tears are waves of oceans
That wash away the need

To hurry, rush, and move along
Just rather, simply, be.

For darling, don't you know them?
Those many mother thoughts

Consumed of you, the whole day through
Nothing could matter more.

Your presence, how it soothes me
I hope, one day, you'll know

Of the way you fill my soul with joy
No matter where you go.

For darling, don't you know it?
The love I have for you?

The way you make me feel complete
By simply being you.

THE PULL

Where you are a planet, I am the sun; your world a solar system anchored around me — the centre, the pull, the light in the dark.

Where you are a flower, I am the rain and the soil; your growth tended by the nourishment I provide — rich, needed, your source of life.

Where you are a lamb, I am the rolling meadows; where you belong, the peaks and valleys of comfort and home.

Where you are you, I am I; mother and child, an innate pairing, devoted entirely, incandescently, in my love for you, rising and falling with the tides of you, for you, my sweet child, forevermore.

BEDTIME

You're clever yes, my little one
You know the days routine

We start, each night, to wind you down
To lead you to your sleep.

You put your arms around my neck
You know this way for sure

I'll listen to you say "outside"
As you point towards the door.

So up and down this driveway
I walk with you each night

I whisper softly in your ear
As my eyes glance at the time.

Yes, it's time for sleep now
Though the sun is still upon us

It's time for you to rest your head
My dear, I will be honest

I love this time just you and I
Your arms around my neck

As I pace with you so slowly
Stopping only when I check

To see if you have left this day
Your eyes closed tight in rest

I sing to you sweet lullabies
Of things that you love best.

We listen to the rustle
As the leaves move in the wind

To the tweeting of the birds
As they welcome nighttime in.

I love this time, just you and I
Your head upon my shoulder

I memorise the weight of you
For soon you will be older.

One day you will not ask me
To hold you in my arms

So I pace with you, in rhythmic step
Your ear upon my heart.

It's getting late my darling
It's nearly time for bed.

It's time for you to close your eyes
And rest your weary head.

I'll walk with you, until you drift
Under the setting sun

I love this time, just you and I
Now sleep, my little one.

HOME AND HAVEN

I watch you, adoringly, as you run toward me
unblinking and with quickened pace

and think

this is the greatest privilege I have ever known —

to be home and haven to another
without consequence or condition.

A place where you can run to
collapse into
trust that from that moment on
whatever it is you feel

will be felt by another.

That you will be welcomed
wanted, accepted
here

always.

Loved, simply

for who you are.

YOU AND I

Before there was a 'you'
There was no you and I

Though somehow, darling, I felt it
As if written in the sky.

I dreamt of you before I knew
The you that you would be

Now here you are, with me now
So new yet known to me.

I look at you and think at times
"I've been here once before" —

Deja vu of a different kind
Of dreams and so much more.

The you that you were meant to be
Is the one that I know now

Watching you in awe each day
Marvelling, wondering... how?

See, it's as if you were meant for me
Your soul at one with mine

And darling, who I was before
Is changing now with time

For now you're here, there's you and I
And suddenly I see

You make me more 'me' than I
Ever thought that I could be.

MY CHILD, MY OWN.

The curl of you against me
The way that we can just 'be'
The softness of your breath
The tenderness you've kept
The joy in all that you do
The confidence to be 'you'
The freedom of expression
The seeking of affection
The smiles while you're sleeping
The hugs when I am weeping
The tiny little features
The way you are my teacher
The love you make me feel
The wonder that you're real
The many things you are
That form the beating of my heart
My child, my own
With your love, I am home.

LOVE YOU FOR YOU

I've loved you, my darling
Since I knew you existed

Since I met you and held you
In my arms as you rested.

I love you, and your smile
And the tears that you cry.

I love your sweet laughter
And your tilted head "why's?"

I love you in darkness
And the light of the sun.

I love you all cosy
And when your wild legs run.

I love you all times
And in all in-betweens.

I love you for showing me
What love truly means.

Darling, I've loved you
From the moment I knew

You existed, my darling
I love you, for you.

two

IN MY ARMS,
IN MY HEART

OF COURSE IT IS YOU

From the very first moment I held you I knew you; who you were, your scent, the feel of you against my skin.

I knew you and yet I had never met you before; a dream I had dreamt a thousand times now here for me to see, hold, land a thousand sweet kisses on.

Real, for the very first time.

I look at you now, and still, I feel you, deep in my soul; as though I have never lived a life without you

as though all along I knew it was you that was coming.

I look at you, and I think, oh of course,

of course it is you.

BABY BUTTON NOSE

Tracing mother finger
Over baby button nose

Silky little lashes
Fall on tiny cheeks of rose

Flushed and warm
Skin to skin

Holding you
Closely in

Memories
And midnight dreams

Of these precious days
Of you and me.

THIS BODY

We sit in the rocking chair, as you flit from left to right, our nightly dance before you drift off to sleep.

Here in the darkness, you rely on touch, searching this body of mine, so new and different to me now, for the landmarks you have known and memorized from the moment of your birth.

Nose against my skin, you coo with delight; the smell of mummy, you are safe here, no need for anything else.

Thrashing side to side, the untameable cub, your energy peaks, bubbling out in raspberries and sweet babbles — the overflow of energy as your little body senses the closeness of slumber.

Your tiny hands push up sinking ever so slightly into my stomach, a mountain on which you can climb, a soft place to land if ever you should need.

With soft breaths you nestle down, burrowing your head into my chest, and instantly you relax; comforted innately by the smell of milk, the soft rhythmic beat of my heart.

Wiggling, you settle in, wrapping yourself in the depths of my embrace, my arms soft pillars of warmth and safety, drawing you into slumber, protecting you from harm.

Your hand reaches my face, the final assessment. "Your nose, mummy?" "Your lips?" "Your eyes are there too?" Fingers placed strategically, exploring the features you already know so well, an anchoring of your own kind.

Darling, in your moments of joy, of despair, of need or want; it is me, this body, that you search for, not entirely aware in your tender age that you and I are not still one.

One last glimpse, as your fingers trace my chin, holding, drifting, wordless

"You're not going anywhere mummy"

Oh my darling, how very right you are.

CURLED INTO ME

As she curled into me
her soft breath warming my skin
she smiled and whispered "mummy".

And then I smiled.

For when I waited for her
longed for her
dreamt of her existence

that is the word

that my heart whispered too.

FAVOURITE TIME OF DAY

I wake each day in search of you
To find you do the same

Half asleep our faces meet
My favourite time of day.

FOOTSTEPS BENEATH THE MOON

Footsteps beneath the moon
Glowing circles in our eyes

Whispering, how I love you too
As your heart beats next to mine.

Silky hands upon my face
Tender kisses upon yours

Rocking in the night's embrace
As the winds release their roar.

Frosted breath sings lullabies
Arms circled, holding tight

Soft sway beneath the starlit sky
As your eyelids drift and wave goodnight.

BEDTIME

Sitting down
Night-time now

Still so much to do.

Hear you cry
Just as I

Start sorting laundry through.

Drop it all
Run and fall

On a random shoe.

Mummy's here
Heart to ear

Breathe and ease into

My loving arms
Safe from harm

Here with just us two.

The dishes pile
But then you smile

They can wait

I'll stay with you.

HERE

Darling, I am here.

When your emotions are big and your understanding of them is small, when the overwhelm peaks and it all becomes too much

I am here

with you, for you, weathering the storm beside you.

When your back is turned, arms flailing, cheeks stained with tears of anger, confusion, need, or want,

I am here

in wait, willing, patient, always.

When you yell for me to go, push me, beg for me to leave you, let you be, I will stay instead

here

steadfast, no want or will to go, I promise you.

And, when the storm passes, and you need me, call for me, reach for me, yearn for my arms to fall into, exhausted

here they will be waiting.

For darling, I love you.

Simply

Wholly

Without condition.

For you, my child

always

'here' is where I will be.

I LOVE YOU I LOVE YOU I LOVE YOU

I love you, I love you, I love you
Over and over again.
My lips rest amidst little whisps of hair
While my tears fall upon your head.

I am here, I am here, I am right here with you
And I promise not to go anywhere.
Holding you closely, your body against me
So you feel in your bones I am there.

I know, I know, I know that you need me
I knew it before you called.
Darling I love you, I feel all that you do
Close your eyes now, and let your tears fall.

I love you, I love you, I love you, my baby
Salty whispers by the light of the moon.
I feel you drift slowly, into a slumber beside me
Your soothing, darling, my soothing too.

CONTACT NAP

This body that you grew in
Your home and haven still.

The place you feel most comfort
The place your body will

Relax into deep slumber
Knowing that I'm here

My breath upon your little face
My heart against your ear.

My darling, how I love it
This time of ours, alone

Your eyes closed tight and dreaming
On the place that you call home.

I'll hold you while you drift off
I'll hold you til you wake

Knowing that it won't be long
Til times sly hands will take

These moments of this little you
When all it is you ask

Is to be held by me in moments
That all too soon shall pass.

REST
UPON ME

Rest upon me child
This place, your first home

This body that you came from
Cushioned waves over buried womb.

Rest upon me, love
Place your ear to my heart

The steady beat that soothed you
Right from the very start.

Come now, rest here now
Again we are one

Moulded back into
The place where you begun.

Darling, stay, rest here
Let your tears cascade down

All that you are feeling
It is shared now, it is ours.

LOOK AT YOU

I hold you as you suckle
And we watch the rising sun

Little gums bulging
New teeth coming to join the fun.

You cried with pain throughout the night
We had such little rest

Hands they danced in circles
As I held you to my chest.

I'd check the clock, "what time is it?"
Twelve, then two, then four

Thought "It'll not be long til morning
And we'll be rushing out the door."

Now, exhaustion hits, I cannot move
I just can't find a way

Pick up my phone, type and send
"Can we see you another day?"

Relief then comes, free to let
My thoughts go back to where

They're needed most, I pull you close
Show you that I'm there.

We'll lay here now together
For as long as you may need

Your body curled up, warm on mine
Your pain now shared with me.

My darling, let those tears out
This time is ours to spare

Close your eyes and rest now
We're not going anywhere.

HOLIDAY SEASON

It's all so loud, it's all so new,
Picking me up, who are you?

Give me sugar, toys and gifts,
Never seen a day like this.

Touch my face, touch my tummy,
Little bit scared, where's my mummy?

"Not happy", "bit naughty",
"Come over here, don't be haughty".

Look around, search the sea,
Faces all so new to me.

Golden light, warmth, and sun,
Locking eyes with my mum.

Overwhelmed, in need of grounding,
Tiny little head is pounding.

Arms around me, safe, secure,
Mummy pulls me in once more.

My head stops thudding, breathing slows,
Need no words, mummy knows.

It is so loud, and it is so new,
Mummy, all I need is you.

WHEN A CHILD NEEDS THEIR MOTHER

You need me

call me

beckon me to provide, soothe, nourish, and care.

My brain ticks; what is it that you need? How can I give, what can I give?

Have it all, whatever you require.

No words needed, a cosmic connection, you and I

linked forever as one, your flesh and soul my phantom limb.

Simply and silently, you surrender to my hold; finding comfort here, an unconditional safety in my arms, on my chest, your place, always.

And here in the dark of night, the midnight hour alone cradling you, I too am at peace; wholly, solely, here with you, present like never before

Realising, as you remind me time and time again; that it is not just you that needs me, my sweet child

but my own soul that needs you too

calls for you

beckons you, always, in return.

THE DAYS OF LITTLE YOU

Back and forth my ankles rock
As they push the chair we're in.

Fan upon us in this heat
We rock with skin to skin.

In the day, you're walking now
'It's gone' I think through tears

In disbelief how fast you've grown
As you begin your toddler years.

Your latest joy is holding things
As many as can fit

Arms so full, you toddle round
Your 'baby-ness' gone now, was that it?

'Time moves fast', 'they grow so quick'
Words until just now

Seeing you change day by day
I truly wonder 'how'?

The strangeness of this 'motherhood'
The want to watch you grow

While also holding on so tight
To the 'baby you' I know.

Now in this creaky rocking chair
As you coo and nurse to sleep

You remind me that you're still so small
I hold you and I weep.

I've learned it now, how quick it goes
So all that I can do

Is soak in every moment
Of these days of little you.

GENTLE WAVE
TO THE DAY

Your hand, soft as silk, sweeps back and forth upon my bare skin,

your gentle wave to this day as you drift off into slumber.

Pulled in close, you curl against me, latched and nestled upon my heart.

You are home here.

Darling, I am home here too.

three

MOTHERING

MOTHER

I see her

Mother

In her ethereal nature

Giver of life

And nurturer

As she moves like the elements

Fluid, floating, a fury and fire

Any and all

When it comes to her child.

I see her

In all that she does

Her contributions

To the majestic

And the seemingly mundane.

I see it

Her love

And her utmost devotion.

Mother

Now, I see her.

THE WAY OF A MOTHER

It's amazing the way
A mother just knows

If her child is ill
Before a sign shows.

It's amazing the way
A mother can sense

The hurt of her child
The moment they tense.

It's amazing the way
A mother can move

When her child is in danger
When there's something to lose.

It's amazing the way
A mother can cry

The tears of her child
From her very own eye.

And it's amazing the way
A mother will hold

Her child in her arms
No matter how old.

It's amazing, it's true
This way of the mother

Where her heart beats as one
With the heart of another.

THE BEAUTY IN
THE IMPERFECTION

I sometimes worry... speaking of them;

the feelings of failure,

the fears,

the fret and the fatigue.

I sometimes worry that verbalizing these less than perfect truths will, in some way, tarnish it — the sacred beauty of my motherhood.

But could it be that in showing them, together, we somehow create something far more beautiful? Like veins within marble, an embracing of the beauty in the imperfection?

A truth that defines it all, in all of its messy brilliance.

A story where, in amongst the tears of joy and gratitude, we shed tears of another kind.

Could it be that, in showing them, we show other mothers their brilliance too, in a truth known only to us —

That of the beauty in the imperfection

of this perfectly imperfect thing we call motherhood.

THE FLAME

So bright
The spark of ignition
For the flame of maternal instinct
Lit without warning
The commencement of it all
With the arrival of them.

The warmth of the pilot light
Floods forward, through blood and bone
Embedding itself into the core of you
Motherhood in its essence
Becoming you, the new you
Kindled, and changed forever.

This warmth
It belongs not just to you
But to your children also
A flicker, a fury
The protector and provider
You are mother now
Forever

An inextinguishable blaze.

I AM BUT 'MOTHER'

'And what is it that you do?' they ask
And I tell them with a smile

I stay at home with you, I say,
'I stay home with my child'.

'And when will you go back then?'
They ask, and raise a brow

'I'm not so sure', I tell them
'My thoughts are in the now'.

I say the years are short
And I'm so thankful for this time

To be able to stay home with you
To have the choice be mine.

Yes, I loved the hard work
The challenges I faced

In the career I earned for myself
The thrill of the rat race.

But for now, the time has come
To immerse in something new

For this thing that they call motherhood
Is important to me too.

I'll have the chance to 'work' again
But not to have these years

Of when you are so little
And so, I think through tears

How grateful I am to have the chance
To sit, and play, and to

Spend this time devoting myself
Entirely to you.

It doesn't pay a cent, this 'job'
But it's the richest I have been

And so, I answer honestly
So that you can see

There's nowhere else I'd rather be
Than here with you, my love

That for now I am but 'Mother'
And for me that is enough.

MOTHERHOOD CV

Hello, yes here it is
What was that? Let me see...

Oh, yes I understand
There is a gap in my CV.

Let me fix that for you now
I'll fill in all the spaces

For though I've not been paid
I've been so many places.

Let me see, oh yes I have
Learned so many skills

Like how to do one handed
Almost any task that will

Inevitably come my way
Be it day or be it night —

And on that note, I've learned as my
Children held me tight

Well in to the midnight hours
The meaning truly of

'Available at all times'
For no time was taken off.

I've learned to build relationships
To nurture others trust

To create, and teach, and care
To find calm in all the chaos.

Yes, I've done so many things
And I've worn so many hats

I've cooked and cleaned and raised
And still I've done much more than that.

I've learned how to surrender
And how to do two things at once

I've learnt how to be brave
And to find courage when there's none.

I've learned what is important
And what can wait a while

I've learned to juggle many things
As I tended to my child.

I've learned how well I function
On such little sleep

I've learned of time's importance
And how together I can be.

Most of all I've learned that
This space in my CV

Is not a space at all
It's filled with skills to keep

And as I list them now
I see one simple thing

That 'motherhood' belongs here —
Let's fill that gap right in.

COMING OVER

'Oh you're on your way?
Sure, that's not a worry

I'm just a little behind
So please, no need to hurry'.

Eyes look to the mirror
And catch my own reflection

Tiny moment of panic
As I end the conversation.

Oh my word, what time is it
Surely not midday?!

'I really need to shower
Honey, can you sit and play?'

Four minutes — timer set —
That's all I have to do

My whole routine — is that the time?
...looks like it's dry shampoo.

Nearly done, little hands
Tap the shower door

"Mummy let me in"
As the timer reaches four.

'Ok then, quickly though
In you come, my love'

I'll give us two more minutes —
I hope that is enough.

Timer sounds, out we get
Now I need to dress

Myself and a now a toddler too —
My gosh, look at this mess.

Clothes are on, whip around
Throwing things in haste

Not sure it's where they even go
But I've got no time to waste.

Look at that, all away
Small pat on my back

Little hands tap my leg
'Oh yes, you want a snack'...

Fridge is empty, mental note
Need to do a shop

Time to get creative —
Find some fruit to chop.

Snacks laid out, water poured
Pop you in your chair

Catch your little smile
As I tame my wild hair.

Take a breath, look around
Count these little wins.

Door bell rings, smile wide
"Hello there, yes, come in!"

NEED TO LEAVE THE HOUSE

I really should leave the house today
It's just that I don't know

How to work the timings out
And when is best to go?

Each hour I say we're going
But then each hour isn't right?

I realize as the minutes pass
That day will soon be night.

Wonder, argh, is it me?
Am I the only one?

Who finds it hard to time it all
And get out in the sun?

It goes like this: "we're ready!"
As your hands move to your eyes

Rubbing them with all your might
I think: "oh dear, nap time".

No problems, we'll go when you wake
I'll be prepared and pack

But darling when you wake
It seems your appetite is back!

Ok then, quick mealtime
And then I swear we'll go

But then you seem to love your toast
And eat it really slow.

Right, that's it! Food is done
Let's get out the door!

One last look around —
Food on the walls and on the floor.

Ok right I'll quickly clean it
Up and then we'll go

Clean it all so ants don't come
And take over our home!

Ok good! Sorted that
Let's put on your shoes

There it goes, the washing's done
Should hang that load out too.

I feel it slowly bubble
That feeling deep inside

That today I've surely failed you
No matter how I tried.

I didn't stop and play with you
Or get you out the door

I'd tell you "yes, we're going soon,
I promise, just one more".

I see your little hands as
They're reaching up to mine

Pointing to the sunshine
"Mama, please, outside".

I drop it all, take your hand
Breathe in as I go

Into the sun, skin so warm
My darling, thank you so

For showing me where it is
I know I'd rather be

This time alone, just you and I
All I truly need

To allow my soul to breathe in deep
My lips to crack a smile

As you spray me with the water hose
And we play a little while.

I thought we should leave the house today
But I watch you run with glee

In the sunshine here, within our yard
And then it dawns on me

That our home is where your heart is
While you are still so small

And all we really needed
Was right here, after all.

STICKY FLOORS

Sticky floors
Overflowing drawers

We only see half the story

Playroom's a mess
Avocado on my dress

Motherhood in all its glory.

Love you too
Banana in your shoe

Little hands around the door

Hungry now
Sibling row

That alone time is no more.

Late to leave
Traffic weave

It's chaos at its best

Little hands
Change of plans

Warm breath upon my chest.

Head is spinning
There's no winning

Though then I win each day

Missed my shower
Picked me a flower

Wouldn't have it any other way.

THIS
TIREDNESS

This tiredness
That brews in our bones
Born from the knowledge
That we are their home.
The giver, the wanted
The always so needed
The safe place, the sanctuary
The calm in each season.
This tiredness
That flows in our veins
Numbed only by love
For these children we raise.
Our fuel, our fire
Our souls walking free
Our joy, our hearts
Our reason, our need.

This tiredness
That aches like no other
Part of the whole
Of the woman called mother.
The aching, the drowning
The arms thrown in want
The pushing, the drive
The coffee by pots.
This tiredness
Part of us all
And yet we push
We do not fall.
For this tiredness
Deep in our bones
Is the proof that we
Are somebody's home.

THE MOTHER, THE MOOR

The mo(or
for their attachment;
secure, unwavering,
a love
like no o)ther.

The mother.

THE SLOWING

Today I was going to be the 'do stuff' mum.
The 'together' mum.
The 'hashtag blessed' filtered photo mum.
Today I was going to get out of the house.
Get some fresh air.
Get out of our own postcode.

But today, I was so tired.
Today, she was so tired.
Today she asked for cuddles, and couch
and, today, that was all I wanted too.

So, today, I embraced it;

the slowing,

the simplest yet most complex act of
surrendering, entirely, to the moment.

Today we stayed at home.
We lay, and cuddled, and wore mismatched
outfits in perfectly unposed photos.
We watched movies, and ate snacks, and left
the mess for tomorrow.

Today, we were 'hashtag blessed'.
Today, I was the 'do stuff mum'.
Just not in the way I had planned...

But that didn't matter one tiny bit.

And if you asked me, I would say

that today, we had the perfect day.

THE MENTAL LOAD

It's the washing and the drying,
the comforting and crying.

It's wiping down the highchair trays,
and putting all the things away.

It's empty pantry, lunchtime orders,
night-time running of bath waters.

Permission slips and dress up days,
costumes for dances and plays.

It's switching out the bathroom mats,
making sure their snacks are packed.

Getting children to the doctor,
booking holidays and adventures.

It's recipes and nutrients,
vitamins and medicines.

Bills and fees and overdues,
and making sure they fit their shoes.

It's taxiing to sports and pools,
researching the local schools.

It's "mum I need's" and "have you seen's",
"don't be late's" and "where've you been's"

It's making sure there's food to eat,
pick up times and meet and greets.

It's finding perfect birthday presents,
and planning all of life's events.

It's "can you get's", and "did you get's",
and "I'm so sorry, I did forget's."

It's being told to fill your cup,
while little arms are reaching up.

It's blowing noses, rubbing tummies,
"it's ok's" and "come to mummy's"

It's holding on to hands so tight
and worrying well into the night.

It's all the things that we do for
the families we so adore

And though, at times, they seem too much
these lists of tasks marked just for us

We know it now, we're not alone
it's what they call 'the mental load'.

ENERGY

Today I was defeated
House was just a mess
Thought that I should clean it up
With the energy I had left.

I looked at you, full of beans
Hands reached out for mine
Pulling me along, "come mummy"
Ah! Tea party time!

I read once of this juggle
Of the 'balls of motherhood'
That some days, they may be hard
But then others would be good.

That the balls all represented
The many different tasks
The different needs and wants
Of the many mother masks.

I remember how it said at times
It's ok to drop a ball.
That sometimes it's important
To know you cannot do it all.

So today I chose carefully
The balls that I could drop
I closed the laundry door
And delayed our weekly shop.

I chose to keep in motion
With what I had today
The balls I would remember
The ones of laugh and play.

I chose instead to muster all
The energy I could spare
To stop and build a fort with you
To drink our tea in there.

For even if some days feel long
I know the years are short
And if there's truly one thing
I've learned from you for sure

It's that, of course, it matters
That I cook and clean your clothes
But what also truly matters
Are the moments between those.

And so I chose that ball to drop
Let the household get away
Chose to lay instead with you
And play the day away.

I was so very tired
You knew it all the same
But you also knew I chose you
I felt it in the way

You leant in close as you laughed
Stars within your eyes
And gave my nose the sweetest kiss
As tears of joy, I cried.

SO TIRED

I'm sorry, I'm just so tired
I'm doing all I can

I wish that I just had some time
To rest my weary head.

I'm just so very tired
I feel it in my bones

I want to play the day away
I hope you truly know

I just can't keep them open
These eyes of mine, you see

They've never been this tired
Or had such little sleep.

I love you, darling, truly
More than you'll ever know

It's just a little tiring
To be always on the go.

I'm sorry I'm so tired
I'm giving all I have

But I see you give all you have too
And so I take you by the hand.

Let's go play, little one
Out in the morning sun

Let me forget my weary mind
As we jump and dance and run.

Now, darling, I'm not so tired
Well, a little still, okay

But when I hear your laughter
The fog, it goes away.

I'm just a little tired
I guess that's part of it

The loving you, the whole day through
Sunrise until sunset.

But you know I wouldn't change it
No wake or yawn at all

Because it's part of mothering
This child that I call

My own, and so I'm tired
So very tired indeed

But I'm tired because I'm 'mother'
The greatest reason there could be.

EXHAUSTION

This level of exhaustion; the one thing no one could've ever prepared me for.

It runs deep in my bones; incessant, unrelenting, anchored steadfast and here for the long run.

It's an adaptation of my body to a way of life once never imaginable; an ability to float sometimes in mere existence through my days, body on autopilot, brain functioning on power save mode.

It's the strange juxtaposition; exhausted beyond repair, silent desires for just four, dare I say five, hours straight, all while adjusting somehow to this constant state of low battery, unable to sleep now even when the chance arises.

Before I became a mother, I thought I knew, and I guess, to some degree, I did.

I knew what your needs would be, and I knew that I could meet them. And I knew from the hours spent watching the waves of you beneath my growing skin, that I would love you.

But what I didn't know was this tiredness, and how capable I would be of navigating it. Waking to you throughout the night whenever you needed, sometimes even before you knew you needed me; our souls innately linked, this secret language of yours and mine.

This drive always to put you first, offer you myself in whatever way you need;

following the intrinsic yearning for you to feel loved, cared for, safe; here with me, always.

This exhaustion, and how capable I am of surviving it, guided by my love for you in this bone aching, deep in my soul, unconditional and unwavering way

something that no one could've ever prepared me for.

Something that I am learning with you, for you, alongside you, my darling,

one moonlit hold at a time.

JUST

It's 'just' one quick task and
It's 'just' another thing

It's 'just' a little longer
Til I join you darling, in

Your play or in your daydreaming
I promise 'just one more'.

I'll 'just' be one more moment
Then we'll walk on out the door.

Darling, I'm so sorry
I feel a lot of guilt

For the way I say 'just' all day
I'll try, darling, I will

To 'just' a little less
And to 'now' a little more.

I know you are so patient
And I see it right before

My very eyes, growing now
Bigger every day

And I just don't want, my darling
To 'just' these days away.

TO MOTHER

To mother
Is to wonder

Am I doing right?

To mother
Is to ponder

Well into the night

If the mother
That I am

Is who you truly need?

If the mother
That I am

Is who I'm meant to be?

But you tell me
You love me

With the way you keep me close

You tell me
To be me

In the only way you know.

Darling
You fill me

With the confidence I need

To mother
You gently

And thanks to you I see

That although
I'm not perfect

You see all that I do

Darling
You show me

That I was meant for you.

HAD TO LEAVE YOU

Today I had to leave you
For the very first time.

Some would call me silly
Others would remind

Me you're now a one-year-old
"It's time you got away"

But your age means not a thing to me
Please, I'd rather stay.

I hand you over gently
As you wave a small goodbye

I promise I'll be back so soon
Do my best to tell you 'why'.

Hesitating at the door
I watch your little wave

Eyes on yours, time stands still
Desperate bids of mine to save

That image of you in my mind
For me to then recall

When a tear of worry wanders down
As I think 'you're still so small'.

I know you're with your grandmother
Whom you so adore

That she loves you as she loved her own
Perhaps a little more.

I know it's only hours
I know it's not for days

But for me even 'a few hours'
Makes me feel I want to stay.

What happens if you cry for me?
What happens when I'm not there?

What if when I return to you
You think I didn't care?

There is no reason when it comes
To a mother and her child

Despite the words of others
It's the heart that leads the mind.

They'll tell me that it's silly
That you will be just fine

But never have I left this club
The exclusive: 'yours and mine'.

I smile with each update
Little snippets sent to me

Floods of mixed emotions as
Part of my heart lives roaming free.

The minutes feel like hours
Hours feel like days

Finally comes the moment
I get to see your little face.

Eyes to cheek your smile floods
Arms spread open wide

Run to me with all your might
My belongings cast aside.

Scoop you up, heart be still
Lungs release and breathe

My baby, back, in my arms
All I could ever need.

WASN'T IT JUST THE BEGINNING?

Sift through it all in your mind, and it's the one that's missing — the storm siren rung by mothers before, warning you of that tidal wave of emotion; of grief, of fear, of disbelief. The end of this era of your life, of which you have emerged bewildered; stunned, dazed, deep from within the trenches.

Words of advice always; chapters upon chapters on the 'firsts': the first few weeks, the first few teeth, watch them as they move — no rest for you now.

Classes, books, mothers before you; "sleep while you can", "soak it in", "it goes so quickly" a dozen

But it's missing; that important part, the chapter of the last.

The last pregnancy, the last birth, the last newborn you will cradle gently through the night, salty tears of exhaustion and gratitude falling softly on their silky skin.

It finds you when you least expect it, this silent grief of motherhood, the closing of one door as the next one opens; a rapid portion of time you are powerless to control.

The trifle of motherhood, complex and multilayered. Grief: that there will be no more. Fear: of the unknown, of having to learn a whole new phase, a whole new you, readjust the idea of who you've become in your mind. Disbelief: that the minutes that felt like hours have become years that felt like minutes.

The strange realization: that you are done.

How did you get here? Wasn't it just the beginning?

TAKING CARE

Midnight hours
Early rise

Tired tears
Cried at night.

Taking care
Us of them

Own care left
Aside again.

Mother's honour
Her heart's work

Little smiles
Show the worth

Of hours given
Tears and sweat

Of times we think
"Not my turn yet".

Just some days
So overtired

In need for just
A little time

To ourselves
Shower, eat

Mornings come
Days repeat.

Look around
Hands up high

Mum friends waving
Side to side

Silent cries of
'We are here

Won't somebody
Lend an ear?'

Drowning in
This need to be

Everyone
And everything.

It takes a village
'True', they say

But where is it
In each day?

Taking care
Us of them

Not one thing
We'd change but then

If we stopped
And saw each other

Would we ask
'Who's got the mother'?

four

OLD FRIENDS, NEW FRIENDS, PLEASE BEAR WITH ME DEAR FRIENDS

BEFORE I WAS A MUM

I want to say I'm sorry
For before I was a mum

For when I thought I had a clue
But really, I had none.

For the times I thought it can't be hard
To just get out the door.

For not thinking how many times
You may have woken the night before.

I'm sorry for my visits
When your babe was but days old

For sitting there for hours
And asking for a hold.

I'm sorry that I wondered
Why it was I that came to you

Not knowing what it takes
Bringing children with you too.

I'm sorry I asked often
When we could catch up

I know now in the early years
'Once in a while' can be enough.

I'm sorry for not seeing
The things you needed so

I've learned it for myself
And now I really know

I should have brought you food
Just dropped it at the door

Told you "There's no need to wave,
But call if you want more".

I should have said I'm always here
There's no need to choose

That you can cancel anytime
No need for an excuse.

I should have left yours sooner
Knowing that for you

Visitors are lovely
But rest is lovely too.

I should've made you cups of tea
Listened to your wishes

Told you "hold your baby"
While I cleaned your dirty dishes.

I wish I didn't ask you
How your baby slept

I wish I had just held you
As you sat with me and wept

Saying nothing to you
As I wiped away your tears

Other than "you're not alone,
They're hard, these early years".

I wish that I had told you
The truth that I now see —

How amazing you are doing
How much you're teaching me.

And so I say with hindsight
And a baby of my own

I'd just do things a little differently
Now that I truly know.

LITTLE CONVERSATIONS

3am, scroll to find
Another just like me

Half awake, I'm pretty sure
But surely half asleep.

Hours now, sitting here
In this rocking chair

The dark of night, wondering
Is anybody there?

Then it comes, that message
"Feed time for you too?"

Heart be still, not alone
Others just like you.

Quick exchange, little laugh
Baby's now asleep

"Got to go, speak real soon"
Back to bed you creep.

Little conversations
Substance, not a lot

But in these early morning hours
As we give all that we've got

These little conversations
Can sometimes get us through

To know that we are not alone
There are others out there too.

LITTLE NOTE

Knock knock knock, knuckles rap
Upon the wooden door

Opened wide to emptiness
I glance around once more.

Creak creak creak, closing now
Suddenly I see

The shining of the fresh tinfoil
Right beside my feet.

Lean lean lean, lift and peer
Into what I've found —

Dinner for tonight
Just left upon the ground.

Tears tears tears, try and see
Who could be so kind

See a little note attached
Warm thoughts, they flood my mind.

Rock rock rock, right to left
Little baby cries

Waddle slowly back
To our kitchen as I cry.

Tap tap tap, type and send
Thank you's, so sincere

To friends who show in many ways
That they are always here.

Eat eat eat, empty cup
Filled now thanks to them

A village of its own kind
In early days postpartum.

Sit sit sit, savour it
This time, just you and I

The gift of dear friends' kindness —
The chance to rest a while.

BEAR
WITH ME

Please can you bear with me
I'm doing the best I can

I know I don't call enough
And cancel all our plans.

I know that not that long ago
We caught up all the time

Called each other often
And chatted over wine.

I know that now I'm different
I seem to pull away

But I'm really still the me you know
It's just that in each day

My thoughts are so consumed
With another person's needs

That I dedicate myself now
To nap times, play and feeds.

It's not that I don't miss it
The banter and the fun

But for now, I'm in the thick of it
After all, she's only one.

So please, dear friends, bear with me
I'm still so very 'me'

I'm just a little tired,
I need you all to see

That one day, all too soon
this little one will grow

I'll be free more then to catch up
Back to the friendships that we know

But for now, I'm in the trenches
And though days bleed in to one

This is where I need to be
While my child is so young.

I may not call as often
I may not have that drink

But know that I'm still here
That, of our friendship, I still think.

That sometimes all I need
Is a hot cup of tea

And a chat with another adult
That understands 'me'.

But my child is so young now
And I am all she needs

At 2am, sat by the moon
I rock her as she feeds

6am, she rises
To the calling of the sun

My energy gone with the night
Day comes and I have none.

Know that I'm so happy now
I feel it in my soul

And I want to share it with you
I want to share it all.

I just ask that you bear with me
Your friendship means a lot

But it's so short, this stage of life
And I'm giving it all I've got.

So, know it's not that I've changed
Or that I no longer care

It's that it's her that needs me
And what I want is to be there.

My friendships mean so much to me
I hope that you can see

All I ask of you, please,
Is to simply bear with me.

CONVERSATIONS

Sorry, I just missed that
What was it that you said?

I have so many thoughts
Scattered in my head.

I really want to focus
I really want to chat

I really want to hear you
It's only just that

I think my brain is broken
Maybe it's on strike

I guess it hasn't slept
As much as it would like.

I'm sorry just one minute
My child has run off

Give me just one second
I don't mean to cut you off.

Ok, good, where were we
Look at me, I'm back!

Sorry, oh you're hungry
Here's the lunch I packed.

Ok go, I'm listening
I really want to hear

Darling, no, sit down please
Mummy needs you near.

I'm sorry, I just missed that
Could you start again?

Golly this is difficult
I remember when

I'd have a conversation
My mind was clear as day

I'd listen so intently
And have witty things to say.

My eyes paid close attention
And my mind was so well rested

Now it's hard to focus
Or even finish my own sentence.

I really want to hear you
I promise that I do

I'm just a little tired
And I'm thinking of her too.

I'm hearing the beginning
But I rarely hear the end

For now, my mind is all for her
I'm sorry my dear friend.

It's just a little hard
To put two words together

I hope you understand
In time it will be better

It's just that she's so little
And my mind is set on her.

I'll do the best I can
To put together words

To listen as you tell me
Right from the very start

But please know it's only short this time
That, well... talking's really hard.

MUM FRIENDS

Mum friends, honestly
How much they get us through

Sipping wine, as children climb
Saying "oh us too".

Minds of those who also know
The daily ins and outs

The push and pull, the highs and the lows
The hardship and the doubts.

The happiness, the loneliness
The love that's like no other

The tiny, little things that matter
Only to a mother.

The joyful tears, the tired tears
The tears cried on the phone

The "oh we really must catch ups!"
While knowing that we won't.

The simple, and the thoughtful
The daily checking's in

The "you can do this" messages
On days we're spread so thin.

The nods of understanding
As we burst in through the door

Hurried, flustered, arms so full
Of babies, bags, and more.

The stifled yawns in unison
The double shot espressos

The glances over tiny heads
The "oh sorry, no, you go's!"

The subtle hands passing you
A baby wipe or two

Unspoken understandings
That some days, get us through.

Mum friends, honestly
They get our mother hearts

That feeling of 'together'
When we're feeling worlds apart.

Oh, mum friends, honestly
I can't put into words

How much they all have raised me
Right from my 'mother' birth.

five

MOTHER, ME

THE BIRTH OF YOU

The birth of my child: definable by no word alone; not one to adequately convey the intensity, the elation, the come down and the fly high.

The tidal wave of emotion; tears founded in joy, in love, from a corner of my soul I never knew existed.

The exhaustion; a tiredness felt deep in my bones, fresh from the battle fields of labour and thrust, without respite or recovery, into the unknowns of new parenthood.

The fear; a sudden newfound and reciprocal fear of mortality — how could she be without me? How could I ever be without her?

The unadulterated joy; pure, enrapturing love — an adoration of those hands, those feet, that moved within me not so long ago.

The small and important details; my new wardrobe of snap release tops, leggings and adult nappies. The ice packs, the waddle, the jelly bowl tummy. The hospital blankets, the clear bassinet, the crying over spilt milk. The visitors, the photographs, the unquenchable thirst. The nurses, the meals, the first cries, the first nappy change — the collection of all the firsts for that matter; both yours and mine.

The feeling, that feeling, of your birth; the beginning of you, the beginning of me also in a sense, the beginning of 'us' as a family. The beginning of a life where time stands still, allowing me hours to observe you, learn you, soak you in; hours that felt like minutes and years all at once.

The birth of you; the moment that challenged any ideas of love I had ever had. Shaking, I bore down, instructed by those around me who had been there before.

"One more, one more and your baby will be here".

That one sentence; a moment in my life too great for words to convey

the gateway to where I am meant to be.

THE TIME WE
NEED TO HEAL

Kettle on, rush a shower, smile as they walk through the door
Hoping they don't see you barely slept the night before.

Accept the thoughtful gift and the coffee bought on the way
Hope your baby plays along, lasts throughout the day.

Feed baby, burp baby, settle baby down
Hand baby over now, hide your tired frown.

Stories, laughs and memories, recounted by each guest
Your ears, they flood with words as they listen for her breath.

Nod and laugh, eye contact, don't forget to smile.
How long since you have held her? Gosh, it's been a little while.

Lunch is done, reset now, time to start again
Feed baby, burp baby, clean the house for when...

Next visitors, here already, just as baby settles
Hand your baby over, watch wistfully as she nestles.

Her smell, her sounds, her little hands, miss her though she's there
Watching others hold her while she sleeps so unaware.

Baby stirs, excuse yourself, sit alone to feed
Wonder when the visitors will give you time you need.

Torn between two different thoughts of pride and want to share
And that of rest and bonding and time for some 'self-care'.

Alarm clock rings, kitchen cleaned, quick mascara on
This is what you should expect, why does it feel so wrong?

Guests arrive, the morning shift, check the clock once more
Knowing that the next will soon be knocking at your door.

Four, no three, hours of sleep as you moved towards her cries
You hold in your determined yawn as you wave the days goodbyes.

Rude, ungrateful, selfish, you shouldn't feel this way
But what will people think if you ask for just one day?

Nappies, burps, feeding times, cries you've yet to learn
Lower yourself gently, grimace with the burn.

Ice packs, pads, pain relief, new to little sleep
Lay your body next to your new child as you weep.

Close the door, curtains down, cancel that next guest
Give yourself the time you need to bond and heal and rest.

Thankful, yes, for their thoughts, intentions pure and true
But you have waited 9 long months, you deserve to meet her too.

MOTHER'S STRENGTH

I have never known a strength such as this

The one given to me by my child.

Her gift upon her arrival

Wrapped neatly with a bow.

'Here now, use it wisely
For it is unwavering, limitless
Unapologetic.'

I have never known a strength such as this

Grown within my womb
Alongside the beating heart of my unborn child

New and remarkable qualities:

To be able to move
Speak
Think
Act

With infallible precision

When it comes to you

Being guided by the womb

That will now never truly be empty

Holding forever it's memories
Of where it all began.

EVERYDAY MAGIC

Sometimes I wonder — is it enough?

Am I creating the childhood I want for you; one of wonder, enchantment, magic?

These ideals of mine, of being able to dedicate, wholly and solely, time to just you, unburdened by the rigmaroles of daily life... simply and sadly, just not always achievable

but slowly, I am realizing that the true magic exists simply as we are

within this mundanity of day-to-day life.

The 'within' — the spontaneous parachutes while folding laundry, the dusting of baking flour upon your nose, the games of chasey down the hallway as we make our way to bed — these moments form this bubble of you and I, in all of its enchanting ever-after-ness.

I see it now that, to you,

the magic is simply my presence,

my attention,

but, most importantly, my inclusion of you in the everyday; actions that show you, you are important, valued, included.

Yes, there will be big memories you hold on to, holidays and birthdays and summer days on the beach,

but all the moments in between

those, I think, you will remember as a whole

a feeling.

You will remember, quite simply, how loved you were

and that to me is pretty magical.

STRONGER

These eyes study me, up and down, closing in, polished silver surface the keeper of great secrets. Who is it that I see?

Those arms, softer, no longer toned from the repetition of weights and long runs on warm summer evenings. Strong now, in a different sense, from holding you, in light bursting energy or heavy deep slumber, my new gym, my new weight.

That bosom, at war with gravity, heavy and needed, no longer solely mine, shared now with another. The source since your emergence of nature's sweetest gift, your comfort and nourishment.

That stomach, with waves that rival the ocean and the resistance of the strongest army, the enemy of denim, once the home of you, where you grew, beneath my beating heart, a place of comfort for you still.

Those hips, reupholstered by biology, thicker, wider, ribboned with earned stripes; ready for you now, a harness and saddle, familiar and fun, natures gift to us, a home for your littleness.

My reflection in the mirror is not as I remember it, shockingly, strangely, altered, for the worse it may seem, but for the better, I am sure.

Changed, yet unchanged,

tangibly and metaphorically stronger than ever before,

having created magic

from within my very own skin.

ALL OF ME

I expected motherhood to be life changing.

But how much so, I'm not sure anyone can truly know until they're in it.

It has thrown me, blind folded, in to the deep end.

It has consumed me in a 'so-incredibly-happy-but-so-incredibly-exhausted' kind of way.

It has demanded every inch of me, mentally and physically.

And yet it has calmed me, soothed me, created within me a reassurance of who I am, who I want to be, who she needs me to be.

It has given me the gift of perspective, and presence, of being able to stop in a moment and simply

be.

And so I give it — all of me

the blood, sweat and tears

happily

and I will do, for as long as I can

because she is all of me too.

My flesh and bones. The blood that runs through my veins.

I give her all of me without even the blink of an eye

because she is all of me too.

SIMPLY AS I AM

You've made me see my beauty
The one I couldn't find

The one I was in search of
In this journey of my mind.

The one I'd always felt that
I'd never really see

Thinking it was just a thing
That would not belong to me.

But you've made me see it through you
As I peer into your eyes

Seeing myself reflected
And stripped of all disguise.

You help me see my beauty
In its truest, rawest form

No need for any makeup
Embracing curves as my new norm.

You help me see a beauty
That comes from so much more

Than how I look to others
As I thought it had before.

You help me see myself in
The way you see me too

A beauty of a new kind
One I never knew

Of fresh face and messy hair
And home clothes every day

Of the comfort that you find when I
Hold you a certain way.

Skin to skin or in my arms
No care of yours is shown

For if I look dishevelled
As we pace these floors of home.

You see a beauty just in me
Simply as I am

Your comfort and your safe place
Your constant place of calm.

I see the way you look at me
In those moments, you and I

And I've never felt more beautiful
Than through the eyes of you, my child.

INSOMNIA!

dear sweet mInd
please be kiNd
let me get some Sleep
this child Of mine
in dreaMs so fine
yet i've Not caught a peep
tIme flies by
she'll surely wAke as I
finally fall asleep!

INSOMNIA!

BREATHE AT LAST

Sometimes I cannot breathe
I fight against the waves

Mouth gaping, soundless, crying out
For somebody to save

My mother mind in routine days
Round and round again

Cook and clean and laundry done
No time left then for them.

Then it comes, a small reprieve
The helping hands I need

Putting on some laundry
Cooking meals for me to feed

My children, all I really want
Is time to spend with them

These hands they help me do that
They help me breathe again.

Floating through the waves I
See the scattered beams

Of the light of someone else
And suddenly it seems

The weight on me, it lifts a little
Lighter than before

I move my feet and suddenly
I am right upon the shore.

Calm around me, resting now
My children in my arms

While another's hands, they care for me
My lungs, they breathe at last.

OVERWHELM

On my feet and rushing round
Yet not a thing gets done

Stood in moments wondering
Am I the only one

Who has these days of overwhelm
Of sitting with blank stare

As children run in circles
Making mess that wasn't there?

I find myself in longing
For the soft and gentle soothe

Of a shower on my own
Or a moment just to prove

That I am still important
My own needs can be met

Cause in the midst of chaos
It's easy to forget.

I stand a little longer
I take a look around

I feel the waves of overwhelm
From the mess in my surrounds.

I'm tired, and I'm unfed
This tank of mine on empty

But when you cry, arms outstretched
And all that you want is me

I see the power of this thing
We know as 'motherhood'

That even when I've thought 'I can't'
Darling, you've reminded me I could.

WHOLE AGAIN

Sometimes I am but pieces

Exhausted

Simply, cntircly.

Effort and smiles, comforting words

No wool for your intuitive eyes.

Your little arms, so new to this world

Surround me

Embrace me, truly, from soul to skin

And

Just like that

I am whole again.

IF I MET HER NOW

Who was that girl, the me I was
Before there was a you?

I wonder if I met her now
I'd see how much she grew.

And I wonder if she met me
She'd like who she'd become

The one she'd always dreamed of
The 'her' that is a mum?

I wonder if she'd like me now
That her that I was then

I wonder if she'd close her eyes
And cry the moment when

I tell her of that day that those
Words flashed on the screen

"Pregnant: 1-2"
The greatest words I've ever seen.

I wonder if she'd understand
The best is yet to come

That when she felt that kick within
She knew who she'd become.

I wonder if she'd cry with joy
Hearing of your birth

How he turned to me, tears in his eyes
"My darling, it's a girl".

I wonder if she'd watch with
Unspilt tears perched in her eyes

The tender rocking of her child
From sunset til sunrise.

I wonder if she'd look at me
And see the her she'd planned

Or would she look at me, just...
Unsure of what happened?

At times I wonder if she knew
Who that her should be

Or if she left it to the stars
And that's how the 'her' is me?

I wonder often if the her
I was so long ago

Would look at me with pride and say
'I really hope you know

I'm proud of who I have become
And honestly I say

I cannot wait to be the you
That I see you are today'.

SELFIES

I go in search of photos
The ones of you and I.

I find them labelled 'selfies'
And I scroll them as I smile.

Often frazzled, never perfect
These rough snapshots of time

May, to others, be imperfect
But are always perfect in my mind.

The unplanned, and the unplugged
The daily range of chaos

The tender and the trying
The truthfulness of us.

They're selfies, yes, I know that
But still, they're photographs

Captured bits of time
Of stolen kisses and baby laughs.

I was told "get in the photo"
And so, I do just that

Ensuring when I'm old and grey
You can still look back

And see the messy hair
And the wide and joyful grin

Knowing that I was there with you
That I soaked each minute in

That all I ever wanted
In these moments of you and I

Was a way to one day show you
Just how hard I tried

To breathe in every bit of it
This sweetest life with you

And so, I take these photos
These little bits of proof

That in between the lovely ones
Nice outfits, best foot forward

Were the snippets of 'normality'
I felt should be recorded.

Sixty thousand of them
All of life with you

Many of them cropped in close
The best that I could do.

I know, love, that these photos
Won't be the best you'll ever see

But they'll show you bits of the 'every day'
That meant so much to me.

Darling, when I lay you down
To sleep by setting sun

My mind still so consumed by you
I scroll through every one

And these images are the ones that
One day I'll say through tears

I'm so thankful for these photos
Of you and I, in your early years.

TIME
WITH ME

Baby asleep
A little while

Should go too
But sit and smile

Snacks in hand
Telly on

Dishes stacked
Care is none.

Should go rest
My weary head

When morning comes
I'll wish I did

But though I'd really
Like to sleep

Just for now
Times mine to keep

And so I sit
A while to be

By myself
Alone, just me.

I AM MOTHER

I am home

I am haven

I am the one that you call out to

I am safety

I am comfort

I am the one who knows the true you

I am strength

I am guardian

I am the grounding in the chaos

I am warmth

I am love

I am the reason when it feels lost

I am who you can come back to

When you're not sure where else to go to

I am home

I am haven

I am mother.

six

IN THE NIGHT

EFFORTLESS

"You kiss her head in your sleep, you know"
"I do?"
"Yes, you do"

Remarkable, isn't it, this pull of motherhood?

This love of unspeakable magnitude; that transcends consciousness or deliberateness,

that calls these forms, yours and mine, to each other; one soul embodied twice.

So entirely enveloping that even in my dreams, when the whole world has fallen away, and all that exist are the creations of my mind, you are there; front and centre.

And as I wake to find the smallness of you curled against me, comforted innately by my presence alone, I see that this, for you, is quite simply

enough.

The innocence of you, your needs and desires, wanting nothing more than for me to love you; with sincerity, and without condition.

With whispers by the moon and the stars, and gentle traces of your eyes and nose as you pace the gates of slumber once more, I assure you, my child, that this is without doubt or hesitation, as natural to me as the drawing of my breath or the beating of my heart.

Loving you, my darling; unwavering and so forever effortless…

I promise you,

I could do it in my sleep.

REST YOUR HEAD WITH ME LOVE

Rest your head with me love
Your breath upon my face

Let the rapid thudding of
Your heart steady its pace.

Rest your head with me love
Lay here within my arms

Let your mind find calm now
With me, you're safe from harm.

Rest your head with me love
Your hands entwined with mine

Anchoring you where you belong
As our hearts beat now in time.

Rest your head with me love
And close your tired eyes

Safe and warm, sleep is near
Sweet dreams now, darling child.

4AM

4am, little mouth
Starts its search again

You and I both awake
You move in closer as

You cry a little, hurting still
Come on teeth, come out!

When oh when will they come?!
We both let out a shout.

Both so tired, both in need
Of a little rest

Oh, my darling, won't you find
Some comfort at my chest?

Nibble, latch, try again
Grimace as you pull

Tiny little drink now
Happy tummy's full.

Lay so still, roll again
Give a little groan

Hand to mouth, back to me
Make sure you're not alone.

Little gums hurt some more
'Mummy, can you see?'

Oh, my darling, yes I know
Come now, lay with me.

Settle in, close your eyes
Whimper as you drift

I curl you in, rock and soothe
Your comfort, mine to give.

Oh so tired, still I wait
For breath and beat to slow

I feel your tension soften
And with that I know

It's my turn now to rest as I
Slowly close my eyes

But wake me, darling, if you need
I'm right here by your side.

BROKEN
LINES

My days once sat divided by
The light of moon or sun

Now the lines are broken
The days roll in to one.

I feel familiar throbs of
That tiredness in my bones

The one of ache and honour
That only mothers know.

These nights, they are so broken
That I along with them

Find myself in pieces
As I wake with you again.

But every time I lift them
My sore and weary limbs

I drift to you on waves of
This ocean that we're in

Where silence falls around us
And we move within the dark

My senses lead me to you
As they have right from the start.

I hold you close, rock and soothe
Remind you that I'm here

My heart beat slow and steady
Beneath your tiny ear.

Darling, it's my privilege
To give this love I've shown

It's just that I'm so tired
In a way I've never known

But laying here, skin to skin
The warmth of you and I

I close my eyes so softly
My arms embrace you tight

Knowing that this time is short
One day I'll sleep again

Darling, let's not rush things
Let's stay here until then.

HAND TO CHEST

Hand to chest, in and out
Feel your rhythmic breath

Fingers to wrist, slow and even
Feel your heartbeats' depth.

Nose to nose, soft as silk
Your eyes closed tight in slumber

Roll back over, close mine too
Try to quiet the thunder.

One eye open, roll abruptly
Check your chest once more

My baby, here, close to me
My heart beat next to yours.

Mutual comfort, you and I
I watch you breathing in.

Incessant worry, sweet relief
The ebb and flow begin.

Love for you, wound into
This newfound mother's fear

Born from me, my phantom limb
Calm only when you're near.

Reach out now, arm on you
Your breath my lullaby

My turn now, lights go down
My darling, sleep, good night.

MUMMY

"Mummy?" I'm right here
Come, hold on to me tight

Im right here, beside you
Within the dark of night.

"Mummy!" You need me
I move towards your call

"Hold me?" I'll hold you
Darling, release it all.

"Mummy!" I'm staying
Now close your tired eyes

Calm now, I'm here now
Warm bodies side by side.

"Mummy?" Yes, darling?
I'm here, you're not alone

Curled in, together
You smile, for you know.

"Mummy", you whisper
As eyelids start to fall

"Mummy", a knowing
A question now no more.

IN THE MIDST
OF SLUMBER

In the midst of slumber, you search for me
Across the sea of mattress and sheet
You move forward, instinctively
My body, the beacon of familiar light, guiding you home.

Softly in the dark I feel them
A small hand on my neck, embracing me, drawing me in
Another hand on my stomach, your home once before, in moments such
as these, I swear you remember
An ear to my heart, the first lullaby you ever heard, each beat for you,
from that moment and forevermore.

Draped across me now the welcome wave of deep sleep laps over you
invited by the tide of safety and comfort, of this unexplainable force that
gravitates child to mother, mother to child.

Sleep, darling, in this place that is yours.

You belong here.

I belong here too.

BIG KING BED

Little feet
Kick blankets off

Little cold
Get some socks.

Big king bed
Not much room

Tiny body
Little spoon.

Mummy here
Daddy there

Toddler limbs
Everywhere.

Left to right
And in-between

Not much space
To be seen.

In the night
Little hands

Out in search
Safe they land

On my skin
Cuddle tight

Oh, how we
Love the night

With little room
But lots of love

Our little one
Right here with us.

I LOVE IT IN THE NIGHT-TIME

Slightest grizzle, not quite roused
Asleep yet half awake

In search of warmth and comfort
From the milk that mummy makes.

Then, as if by magic
Through the dark her arms appear

And pull me in to where it's warm
I smell it, milk is near!

It wasn't far to go at all
She was right next to me

She tells me that she loves me
With little kisses on my cheek.

I love it in the night-time
When all the lights go out

I reach my hands in to the dark
And as they wave about

They land upon the people
That smell and feel like home

I rest my head on mummy as
My toes find daddy's nose.

I cuddle in, where's that milk?
Hold on to her tight

Rest my feet on daddy and
Drift back into the night.

I love it in the night-time
Warm arms and milky dreams

And those that smell and feel like home
Right here, each side of me.

BUTTERFLIES OF SLUMBER

Lashes dance like butterflies
Upon your sleepy lid

Breathing slow and steady
As slumber makes its bid.

Curls cascade and frolic as
You shake your head once more

Your little mind so busy
As it paces slumber's door.

Babble, pull, quick request
My arms they hold their place

Singing you sweet lullabies
Landing kisses on your face.

Off you go now, little one,
Close those heavy eyes

Relax into this moment,
Your heart beat next to mine.

Nestle in, let lashes land
Your eyes they close so tight

Your curls rest soft upon my arm
As you gently greet the night.

ALWAYS BE YOUR HOME

I wake to arms in search of me
A smile upon your face

Contented from a restful sleep
With us, in your safe place.

Cheerfully, you point outside
Delighted as your ears

Hear the early morning song
Of birdies far and near.

I listen as you babble
Excited for the day

We wake together slowly
As if there is no other way

And it feels so very long ago
They swaddled you so tight

And placed you in that plastic crib
Beside me in the night.

They told me it was best, my love
To give you your own bed

But this heart of mine, it wanted
To keep you close instead.

All distress would fall away
when ear was placed to heart

The sound of me, all you've known
Right from the very start.

We knew it in those moments
Where you were meant to be

Only small, for so long
You curled in next to me.

For we were one, you and I
I swear that we still are

As if your tiny body
Is made of fragments of my heart.

You lay your head upon me
As if to say you know

Not long ago you grew here —
It will always be your home.

seven

MILKY BREATH

MILKY BREATH

Milky breath

Silky hands

The warmth of you

Against me as

You drift to sleep

While I drift too

Comforted

By glowing moon.

Warm soft cheeks

And steady breaths

The night-time seeking

Of my breast.

Heavy eyes

Softened grasp

Slumber rolls

Over us.

Night-time, darling

You and I

Together, here

Til morning light.

SUNSHINE

Lay here in the sunshine
The warmth upon your skin

As little lips drink mothers milk
Like sunshine from within.

Lay here in my arms now
Your heartbeat next to mine

As we listen to the sounds of birds
Sweet natures lullabies.

Lay here with me, darling
Beneath deep shades of blue

As toes they tickle fields of green
A grounding, me and you.

HOW LONG?

I scroll through those old photos
As you have your nightly feed
Beginning at your birth
As you crawled on me in need.

Nature's draw, newborn's call
Mouth to breast at last
1 week old, then 2, then 3
I scroll throughout the past.

Feeding so much harder then
So new to you and I.
If only I had known then
As I held you and I cried

Begging in the dark of night
That you and I would match
Shields and pumps and milk-stained tops
New holds to help you latch.

Yes, if only I had known then
What it is that I know now —
That this would one day work for us
That we would both learn how.

That once we worked together
Past the pain and stress and tears
That what it is that we would find
Would be magic for some years.

So when we're asked how long it is
We think that we will go
I say it's been a journey
I say it's hard to know

I say how much I love these times
Alone, just you and I
That there's no magic number
No end date in our minds.

I say that we've worked hard at this
Together, just us two
That you are still so small and
That, my darling, it's up to you.

LATCHED IN SLUMBER

My phone dropped out of reach
As I lay right next to you

You lay there latched in slumber
And I wondered what to do.

Glancing down I saw them
Your hands upon my chest

Your lashes dancing daintily
Round eyelids as they rest.

I saw your little nose
And your perfect little cheeks

I saw your little lips curl
In motion as they feed.

Just like that I lost it
The want to seek and find

The phone no longer mattered
More than memories of the mind.

I curled myself around you
Got lost in mother's wonder

As I lay with you beside me
Asleep and latched in slumber.

OUT AND ABOUT

Hand it waves
Over my chest

Gone in search
Of milky breasts.

Touch your hand
"Yes I hear"

Glance around
See who's near.

Lower you
Let you latch

Eyes dart round
Right and left

Seeing who
Is watching then

Down they go
Once again.

There they are
Little eyes

Calm, content
I realize

Nothing matters
Except you

Others thoughts
Mean nothing to

Me when it is
You who calls

So with that
My guard, it falls.

Suddenly
I'm less aware

Of strangers' eyes
As they stare

At you and I
As you feed

For in that moment
All you need

Is mother's milk
And warm embrace

And so I focus
On the face

That looks for me
When in need

Darling, as you lay
And feed

For every chance
That I get

To hold you, feed you
I forget

The eyes of others
Around me

I see just yours
With that, I'm free.

SIDE TO SIDE

"Goodnight, darling" I whisper
As your eyes flutter slowly

Your latch still intact
As I hold you in closely.

"I love you", I murmur
As I lift you in the air

Switching you from right to left
Where you feed without a care.

"Goodnight, my love, I'm right here
If ever you should need"

I whisper to you gently
As we close our night-time feed.

Leaning down, I kiss you
Gently on your head.

A final show of love as I
Lay you down in bed.

My darling, many years from now
I hope it all remains

These feelings of my love for you
Each time I spoke your name

And how I moved you softly
As we danced from side to side

The tenderness with which
I held you through the night.

One last glance upon your chest
The rise and fall once more

And I whisper how I love you
As I gently close the door.

LITTLE MOUTH

Little mouth in search of milk
Open to the air

Silky little hands join in
Waving here and there.

"Mummy" muttered with such might
Body shuffles close

Moving well within the night
Led by seasoned nose.

Latch and lay, here we are
Head upon my chest

Little hand waves in thanks
I hear your steadied breath.

Savouring this moment
As you sleep so soft and sound

You smile in your dreams, my love
For mother's milk you've found.

MASTITIS

The familiar wave of tiredness
As it travels through my bones

They ache together in pain
As if they already know.

Feeling nauseous, skin so warm
I lift my top to see

The redness I expected
As infection takes hold of me.

Ache and cry, awake all night
Shower seven times

You curl your little fists as I
Bite down hard on mine.

Massage, feed, warm heat pack
Do all that I can

To clear the dreaded mastitis
To feel healthy, once again.

Sleep and rest, pain relief
Feeding on both sides

Working as a team now
Together, you and I

To fight this little battle
To meet it at the source

To do all that we can while
Mastitis runs it's course.

PUMPING

The familiar humdrum
There it goes

Eh oh eh oh
Let down flows.

Pumping pumping
All day long

Topping up
Freezing some.

Pump and clean
Sterilize

Pack it up
Til next time.

Round and round
And round it goes

No one told me
Didn't know.

Pumping pumping
In between

Feeds in case
We are in need

Of mother's milk
For baby's mouth

Hungry, top ups
Mummy's out.

Eh oh eh oh
Puff and pull

Pumping til the
Bottles full.

Hands were busy
Now they're free

Pumping bra
Attached to me.

Familiar humdrum
There it is

Pumping pumping
Just like this

For mothers milk
And baby's call

Pumping now
Please don't fall

Bottle oh
I beg of you

Stay upright
What would I do

If hours spent
Fell to waste

And little tongues
Don't get to taste

The drops we worked
So hard to get

Surely, I would
Have to let

Tears fall down
But if not then

I'll stay here pumping
Once again

Knowing with
Each push and pull

Each freezer bag
That is now full

I'm doing all that
I can do

To store sweet mother
Milk for you.

131

LITTLE
ACROBAT

Little acrobat
Legs up in the air

Downward dog, wiggle round
Legs go everywhere.

Milky time, you and I
Mouth to breast you go

Drinking all you can while
You move round to and fro.

Spin around, sitting now
High on mummy's head

Filling up your tummy
Before it's time for bed.

Push and pull, chew and bite
Head throws left to right

A little pup upon her mum
You thrash with all your might.

Darling child, how I smile
(Sometimes grit my teeth)

At your acrobatics
And the way you wave your feet.

Long ago you lay so still
Here within my arms

Now I close my eyes and hope
Your teeth will do no harm!

Darling, how I love you
And how I love the way you play

In these quiet moments
Within our everyday.

It means that you are growing
And I am growing too

It means that we are still here
On this journey, I with you.

I GREW FOR YOU

These mounds of me
This home of you

The skin in which
Your body grew.

The place your head
Now softly rests

As mouth it moves
Towards my breast

And little hands
As soft as silk

Knead as one
For mummy's milk.

Eyes they drift
Like butterflies

Closing slowly
As you lie

With feet at rest
On fleshy waves

Where you once grew
Where life was made

And now I see
My darling child

As we mould here
Just you and I

These mounds of me
Were made for you

You grew in me
I grew for you.

eight

OTHER LOVE

ONE DAY YOU WILL KNOW

She whispered softly to me
With tears perched in her eyes

"One day you'll know a love like this
A love as strong as mine".

Gently she released me
Watched my travels from afar

Reminding me, always
I was the beating of her heart.

And through the years she'd say to me
Each and every time

"One day you'll know the love I feel
For you my darling child".

Then when she heard the news she'd yearned
A child was on the way

She said to me once more with love
"You will know one day".

Now here I lay, a mum myself
A baby of my own

Relying on my mum once more
Forgetting that I'm grown.

And as I kiss my baby's head
Within the dark of night

It's then that I think to myself
"Dear mother, you were right".

I cradle my sweet baby
Whisper softly in her ear

"Your Gigi said one day I'd know
And that day is finally here".

THE CENTRE
OF IT ALL

You are the centre of it all.

Before you we lived together, parallel, and yet entwined, two individuals who chose to share an existence; content, happy, yet free to change direction if and whenever we pleased.

Now that you exist, we find a new version of 'us'; pulled into orbit, centred now by the gravity of you.

You have changed us, both as individuals and as a couple; perpetually bound by purpose, bound by the shared experience of parenthood, bound forever by the pure existence and adoration of you.

You, our baby; our joy, our driving force, our reason now for it all.

This version of us, now,

for and because of you.

WHEN I HUG MY MOTHER

A tear moves down my cheek as
Her arms embrace me tight

I think of you suddenly
As the day rolls into night.

I think of how you look at me
The way I look at her

A look I never understood
A look that has no words.

I think of how you close your eyes
Longer than before

When I greet you with a hug as
I walk in through the door.

I never really noticed
I guess I never tried

To see those little signs of
Your love throughout my life.

Of course, I knew you loved me,
I just never knew how much

Until I had my daughter
Until I felt this love

And now I know that feeling
The skipping of your heart

When your child's arms embrace you —
Your soul's missing part.

I know it now, how it is
The smallest things to me

Are still all special 'firsts' for you
No matter what my age be.

I watch your eyes fill with tears
In moments that to some

May seem so insignificant
But never to a mum.

Yes, I see it clearly now,
The way you look at me

As if you're still amazed
As if you can't believe

That this person standing right here
Before your very eyes

Once lay beneath your heart
Heard it beating from inside.

I see it now mum
Because now I feel the same

This feeling of wonder
Every time I call her name.

I understand the reason
That you linger more each time

A child of yours holds you
For I do the same with mine.

US

The way you look at me
is changed, yet still the same

The way your voice steadies
when your lips sound out my name.

Embedded in you now
as expected as your breath

My name a first reaction
in sickness and in health.

Familiar now, you and I,
no longer are we new

Funny how, now we're three,
we forget when we were two.

But there are, of course, the moments
like passages of time

Glimpses of the reasons we
became both yours and mine:

Quick glances and hand grazes,
pure joy from this shared laughter

We are two together
as we marvel at our daughter.

No longer who we were before,
nor want to be again

For we are changed because of her,
better now than we were then.

It takes some time to learn the new,
the 'we' that we are now

Sometimes we feel like strangers,
at times we wonder how?

But once we had a reason
and that reason still remains

Now we have another
and that reason has a name.

With tired eyes we wonder
as we wade through our first year

Parents now together, but are we still us?
Yes, we're still here.

HER GRANDMOTHER, HER FRIEND.

You see me now
As you once were

You see me now
When you look at her.

Your baby a mother
To a baby of her own

So grateful to you
For the love that you've shown.

You love her so deeply
As if she is yours

And at times, I think
A little bit more.

You clap and delight
In all that she does

Hold her when she needs
Or just because.

It lightens the soul
Knowing that you

Love her as I do
And you're there for her too.

Her eyes light up
When you enter the room

Cries when you leave
"Darling, she'll be back soon".

I listen through walls
As you laugh and you play

Her time with you
Her greatest of days.

She loves you so dearly
And I know just why

She feels how you love her
She feels how you try.

I see her surrender
So safe in your arms

Her grandmother, her friend
Oh, you have her heart.

THE ONE THAT WE CALL HOME

Who we were and who we are
Different as can be

A world of new beginnings
And a world of memories.

Looking back at photos
Almost strangers in my eyes

A life that feels so distant
Divided by the lines

Before and after, then and now
The way that we now view

This life since the arrival
Of our dear, beloved, you.

Beauty then and beauty now
Though reasons not the same

Before we sought a feeling
Now the feeling has a name.

I look back now and realise
We thought life was complete

Before we held you in our arms
And you brought us to our knees

In wonder and amazement
This life of yours, for us

The life that we had lived before
All part of the path

To who it was we're meant to be
And now, darling, we know

It led us here to you, our child
The one that we call home.

NEED YOU

I need you mum, I'm only so small
a baby, dependent, for you I will call.

I need you mum, school bag bigger than I
holding your hand, wiping tears from my eyes.

I need you mum, pacing the halls
of highschool still need you to guide me through all.

I need you mum, as I pack up my room
the first time I'll sleep under my very own roof.

I need you mum, as I cross the stage floor
to accept the degree I've worked so hard for.

I need you mum, as I battle my nerves
excited but anxious for my first day of work.

I need you mum, the first that I tell
the moment we know there will be wedding bells.

But I need you mum, more than ever before
as I hold my own child, who I've long waited for.

As the pattern starts over, one thing remains true
no matter my age mum, please know I need you.

OH, MY HEART

I watch him sway you gently, rocking side to side.
Your eyes drift off slowly. His face fills with pride.
He loves you oh so deeply, you love him in return.
I've seen it when your eyes meet, from the moment of your birth.
Now as I watch him hold you, the tear fall makes its start
His love for you — so pure and true

my heart, oh, my heart.

TO MY OWN MOTHER

To my own mother,

Who carried me, carried within her this heart of mine, that beats now in turn for a child of my own.

Who has shown me a love that, no matter what in life, assures me I have unconditional and undying support; a safety net always, there to catch me if I fall.

Who has celebrated, or mourned, everything, with me, for me; herself knowing the sunshine of my happiness, and the aches of my hurt, feeling what I feel, innately, forever and always.

Who has loved me with a love that has persevered, without shame, into adulthood, with the same ferocity, honesty and sincerity it existed when she held me in her arms those few, but many, decades ago.

Who has been, and in turn has shown me how to be, unashamedly, unapologetically, 'mother' first and foremost, with no age or circumstance bringing expiration to that.

Who has shown me a newer love, the one of hers for my child, otherworldly, as if plucked from the stars above in its magnitude and magnificence.

Who has taught me, with her love, how myself to love, with the same intensity, and sentimentality as her own beautiful heart.

Who has taught me everything, for that matter.

I love that when I speak the word "mum", my meaning is you.

MY DEAR FRIEND,
THE MOTHER

It has changed her

loving you.

It has made her wiser

and lighter

and brighter.

She cries more too, which is new.

Yet, at the same time,

she remains completely unchanged.

Content wholly and solely in the comfort your love provides her

to be completely who she is meant to be.

TRAVEL TIME

Her eyes the portal for you
A glimpse of days gone by

You gaze a little longer
As she toddles past you while

You play together, you and her
Content within your pair

Your time together gifted
As if no one else is there.

I see it every now and then
When your mouth sounds out her name

The glimpses that you see
Of her and I the same.

And every now and then
I hear it, soft and fleeting

The accidental name —
Your past and present meeting.

Her name and mine blended
For you within your mind

The presence of my child
A portal back in time.

I hold on to her dearly
In these days of little her

Knowing that they're borrowed time
As days become a blur.

But you show me in your love as
The mother of the mother

That someday in this life
I may love another

As much as I love her now
And so, I sit a while

With tear drops falling softly as
I watch you travel time.

MY HUSBAND, YOUR DADDY

Can you feel it? The way he loves you, watches over you, considers you in all that he does?

Can you feel his joy as he takes note of your growth; "she loves that toy, this song, look, she's found her toes now". The glimmer in his eyes when his gaze crosses you; pure happiness, so palpable, I've never seen him quite like this before.

Can you feel his heart beat faster and slower all at once as he shares those things most special to him; watching as you smile, delighting in your glee. A contentment of the heart; effortless and mutual.

Can you feel the care he takes; so soft with you, his little one, gentle with you always. Even in his play, I feel it, ensuring in each moment you are safe, protected, loved, undoubtedly so.

I would say you've changed him, but that's not entirely true.

From the moment you drew your first breath it seems you have merely awoken a part of him that even he did not know existed.

An addition to the man I already loved, the beginning of the truest version of him.

Can you feel it?

Because I can.

I feel it deep in my soul, with every move he makes and word he speaks, that the greatest gift life has ever given him

is you.

FATHER

You are strength
You are steadfast

The calm within the season.

You are kind
You are patient

The constant voice of reason.

You are provider
And protector

The shoulder that we lean on.

You are observer
And supporter

The one who'll always be on

The sideline
The frontline

Or whatever side we'd rather

For you are loving
And you are so loved

You are my daughter's father.

nine

INTUITION

ALL I HEARD WAS YOU

I think of all the things that they
Said that I should do

"Have the room 18 degrees
And have it pitch black too."

"Have her close enough to see
And close enough to touch

But do not bring her in with you
No, that's far too much."

"Wrap her tightly, arms tucked in
White noise playing loud

Then place her drowsy but awake
And leave without a sound."

As I lay here holding little you
Asleep within my arms

I think of all the things I wish
They'd told me from the start.

That when you cried, that was you
Calling out in need

That no matter why you called
The answer would be me.

That your body was not long from mine
You'd miss the steady sound

Of the heart that beat above you
As you curled yourself around

The warmth of mother waters
Held in by the embrace

Of mother skin, that grew for you —
The place that kept you safe.

That night-time wouldn't change a thing
Your calls still meant the same

That you wouldn't know the sun had set
As your lungs cried out my name.

That, darling, we weren't broken
That this is how it should be

That the nights they might seem long
But the days fly by so quickly.

You see, they didn't tell me
But my heart knew what to do

It told me just to listen
And all I heard was you.

FROM THE ROCKING CHAIR

I'M RIGHT HERE

Lights out, dummy in
Find my loving hold

Winding down slowly
From the evening tales told.

Wiggle in, bury deep
Block out all the light

Lift your hand, search my mouth
Try with all your might.

Pinch my lashes, then my nose
Stroke my chin and cheek

Know that I am here
Providing comfort that you seek.

Breathing slows, hands still raised
Resting on my face

You turn with force and speed at once:
"Good! No one has filled her place".

Your dummy's out, lifting up
Your new and favourite game

I rock and sssh, dummy in
Gently say your name.

Flash a smile, nestle in
Eyelids start to fall

Feeling in your bones my love
My giving of my all.

"Put her down", "You'll spoil her"
"Rod for your own back"

Words from those around us
As I rock you on my lap.

My turn now; nuzzle in
Breathe the scent of you

Shuffle as your body
Stretches over where you grew.

Shut them out, pull you in
Let you know I'm near

This time so short, just you and I
Sleep now, mummy's here.

FEED TO SLEEP

"You mustn't give the breast
To calm that child down"

She says through furrowed brow
And a tired old frown.

"You're just a crutch, don't you know
She'll never learn to soothe

If you carry on holding her
And offering the boob".

These words of others echo
On walls of quiet rooms

As I hold you in my arms
And you feed until you soothe.

Darling, do you feel it?
That soft and gentle lull

Of warming waves and mothers chest
As dark of evening falls.

Feed to sleep, my child
Yes, close those tired eyes

Your comfort and your calming –
Such treasured gifts of mine.

No want or word of others
Mean more to me than you

So, I listen for your cries
To tell me what to do.

Now, close your eyes my darling
For slumber, it awaits

I'll hold you as you drift there
On warm, sweet, milky waves.

VULNERABILITY

I let you see me cry

tears of

happiness

sadness

gratitude

hurt

so that you may know I am human
and that, at times, I cry too.

I let you see me process

experiences

and emotions

so that you may learn ways in which
one day you may process too.

I let you see me vulnerable

so that you may see the strength
that exists in vulnerability.

I let you see me feel

in the hope it will breed
a strength within you

to be ok with feeling too.

CRYING

You're crying darling, so am I
For when you cry my heart cries too.

Each sob of yours, felt in me
As waves that ripple through.

For we are one, you and I
Your birth changed not a thing

And it matters not how fast you grow
For you still grew once within.

Yes, when you cry, child of mine
Please know that I cry too.

Your joy is mine to share
Just as my heart, it aches for you.

In moments that you're feeling pain
Or sadness or despair

I need not hear your words for me
To know your pain is there.

I hold you tight, wait for calm
As long as you'll allow

Beg the waters of my cries
To cleanse your pain somehow.

You're crying darling, so am I
My heart, it aches for you.

My child, all you feel inside
Please know I feel it too.

CLUNG TO ME

You clung to me
White knuckled and desperate
Pulling into me
Panicked efforts
To feel my closeness
To be one once again.

You clung to me
As I held you tightly
Hoping
Begging
For your fear
To fall into me
Be mine
Not yours
Ever again.

You clung to me
And I held on to you
Tears of mine
Entwined with yours
Not quite realizing
As you clung to me
Fear stricken and calling
That, my darling,
I clung to you too.

HUMAN

Tears roll down your little face
And they mirror, love, on mine

For the tears you cry become mine too
No matter age or time.

I let them fall so freely
As I hold you close to see

That tear fall is ok, my love
In times you truly need.

That crying is just part of it
Being human, darling, and

I will not say to stop
I'll try my best to understand.

I'll hold you as you cry
And I will listen when you speak.

I'll show you that it's strong to cry
When others say it's weak.

I'll let you see my own tears fall
To balance out the smiles

To show you though we're happy
We all get sad once in a while.

All I hope to show you as
I hold you close to me

Is that you, too, are only human
And you can cry, darling, if you need.

BRAVE

As the needle cut
I saw your tears well

Your bottom lip dropped
As the first one fell.

And I remember it clearly
The smile she gave

As she said to you quickly
"Come on now, be brave!"

I held you in close
As you held your breath in

Cheeks stained with a gloss
A red tint to your skin.

"You are brave" I whisper
"Just as you are

For its brave to tell mummy
How you feel in your heart.

It's brave to let tears fall
Rather than sit in your eye.

It's brave to tell mummy
The fear you feel inside.

It's brave to seek out
Some comfort or touch.

It's brave to tell mummy
When it's all a bit much.

Darling, you're brave
I promise you this

Because telling me how you feel
Is the bravest brave there is."

SAY NO

'No' your head shakes softly
As your eyes they lock with mine

Telling me, as best you know
That I am needed by

The way you stare, stern and still
Your voice, it makes no sound

And just with that, I move to you
Collect you, arms thrown round.

Voice, it stays so silent
Eyes stay locked with mine

Safe here now, within my arms
We feel the slowing time.

Nothing else now matters
But what you have to say

And if your voice feels quiet, then
We'll find another way.

For it's your right to say no
If and when you please.

Darling, take your time now
I'm right here if you need.

CHILDHOOD

I wonder why we rush them
When all we ever say

Is "oh to be a child!"
As we watch them in each day

Living as I'm sure that we
All wish that we could live

Soaking in each moment —
These lessons theirs to give.

A freedom of their own kind
To say and do with ease

What their heart desires
Or as their own mind's please.

So, I wish we'd let a child
Just be a child while they can

For once these days are over
They'll not be had again.

No, there is no need to rush them
In fact, let's beg them, please, to stay

Let's guard them with our lives
Their precious childhood days.

THE COMFORT

I've seen it now, each time you're sad
How when you are with others

You go in search of eyes you know
For the comfort of your mother.

You turn to me and run as
Your arms stretch open wide

Tears stream down your little cheeks
As you sob through tiny cries.

It's not that you don't love them
Or their love needs to be earned

It's that our hearts still beat as one
A skill that can't be learned.

Your pain needs no description
I know it all at once

I know just what you need from
The very moment I see you run.

And as your arms connect with mine
So quickly do you soften

This pain you feel, just yours no more
It's shared, then soon forgotten.

I hope you know that times like those
The world goes out of focus

And all I see, right then, is you —
Forget the world around us.

My love, I promise, forever
Until the end of time

My eyes will always search for yours
And, darling, your arms can always reach for mine.

MOVE TO YOU

"Listen here, leave her now
Why don't you let her cry?

She's had her feed already
You changed her, so she's dry."

I slowly fade the sound out
Lips move without a sound

My arms, they move towards you
As if nobody's around.

This cry of yours, I feel it
So deep within my bones

Your only way of saying
"Please help me" — don't they know?

Your body moulds against mine
As mine moves far from them

The sobs of yours peter out
You're calm now once again.

Fed and dry, yes, but if you cry
Please, let it be with me

Folded here within my arms
Where you are meant to be.

Please know, my child, when you cry
I'll always move to you

For darling, you and I are one
Your tears are my tears too.

LOST HERSELF

'She's lost herself', they say
As they talk with one another

'She's nothing more now
Than a wife and a mother'.

'Her kids are her life' they say
Their heads bowed down in whisper

'I wonder if it's noticed,
If people even miss her?'

'Make sure to find some you time'
They say with tilted head

Expressions speaking volumes
Of the silent words unsaid.

They think that I am lost, I know
Gone now with the season

But oh, how wrong they are
I came here for a reason.

My darling it's my choice, you see
To focus so on you

But then again, perhaps it's not
I felt it as you grew.

Yes, just as all the other things
The beating of my heart

The need to breath, the flow of blood
I loved you from the start.

I knew it from so early on
This stage of you and I

Would move so very quickly
Blink as it passed us by.

I made the choice right then and there
To take this borrowed time

To surrender to the magic
In this life of yours and mine.

My child, they may say it
That I've lost myself to you

And I guess in many ways
That what they say is true.

I've lost myself, yes, they're right
The 'I' I was before

For 'I've' become a newer me
A me that I like more.

My darling, you have given me
A strength I've never known

A trust within myself
To protect us as we've grown

A tender love and thanks
For this body in which you grew

My mind a place of calm
More so now because of you.

No, with you, my love, I am not lost
I'm right where I belong

I only truly found myself
The day that you were born.

TODAY

Today I did so little
I barely got us by
I woke up to your little tears
And held you as you cried.

I rocked you as the pain moved
Through your body into mine
Catching all your tears as
I sung you lullabies.

I gave you all the food that I
Could make with just one hand
Lay with you upon the couch as
You lay upon me and

Stayed there for some hours
As you drift off then to sleep
Nap time there upon me
Your pain then mine to keep.

The laundry sat untouched and
The kitchen was a mess
But you told me with your eyes
That all you needed was my chest

To lay your head upon as
You listened to the beat
Of my heart below your ear
Felt the warmth upon your cheek

And so, we lay for hours
On that couch, just you and I
As I rocked you and your tears fell
Until they all ran dry.

Darling, I thought I did so little
But I gave you all I've got
So, when I really think of it
Today I did a lot.

A NEED ALL
OF ITS OWN

Sometimes there is no 'reason'
Nothing at all to 'fix'

Sometimes it's simply needing
A closeness just like this.

The wanting of some arms wrapped
Around you, warm and tight

In whispers or in silence
In day or dark of night.

Sometimes there is no blank line
Or need that's not been met

Sometimes it's simply wanting
The closeness that you get

From the arms of those who love you
Holding you in close

Heart to heart, and skin to skin
A need all of its own.

THE BOOKS SAY

The books say to put you down, drowsy but awake and so I rock you to sleep in my arms instead.

The books say to avoid eye contact, no talking, don't stimulate the baby and so I hold you close, look deep into your eyes, stroke your cheek, whisper to infinity how much I love you instead.

The books tell me what time you should go to bed, how long you should sleep, how long you should be awake and so I watch you, learn the subtle rub of your eyes, the shift in your breath, your mood when you wake, let you guide me instead.

The books tell me you shouldn't need me, you should be independent, you should learn to self-settle, so when you cry, I bring you in with me, let you relax into my presence, my warmth, do the settling for you instead.

The books tell me so many things about you and yet I do not to listen

for these books have never met you, my sweet girl...

They don't know you like I do.

SURRENDER

The greatest gift I gave us
Permission

The unshackling of my mind
Allowing

My inner instincts to reign
Releasing

Me from the should do's and the should not's
Providing

Myself, my child, the lightness of trust in 'us'
Freeing

Our sacred time of the chains of stranger's thoughts
Ensuring

All we hear is our own sound, the silent beat of two hearts as one
Immortalizing

These feelings; free from angst, doubt, regret
Granting

Myself, and my darling child, this release
Collapsing

With relief into what we felt to be right all along
Surrendering

To the raw, the trying, the remarkable; to these early days with you.
Drifting

As I surrender; I am free; we are free
Blissfully.

WATCHING
YOU GROW

SLOW DOWN, TIME

Slow down time
Where is it that you go?

It's feels like only yesterday
I dreamed how she would grow.

Her little feet inside me then
Kicking left and right

And now I lay beside her
As she drifts into the night.

It's as if suddenly
Her little self has grown

Laughing, talking, running now
If I only I had known

That while some days had felt so long
Or the same as each before

Almost as if overnight
My newborn would be no more.

So, I think to myself as I watch her
Little arms move in search of mine

That this moment one day too will pass
And, oh, how I wish I could slow down time.

THE OCEAN

I watch as tears
Well up high

Promising
To leave my eye.

You splash and squeal
In delight

Reach out high
Hold me tight.

Ocean laps
Upon our feet

Sand and sea
Dance as they meet.

My darling how
You love it so

The sound as waves
Roll to and fro

The feel of sand
Between your toes

The warmth of sun
Upon your nose

The wonder of
This world you see

The one that you now
Share with me.

And darling how
I love it too

These moments I
Cherish as you

Show me what
It means to be

Content and present
Wild and free.

Time stands still
I listen now

So heavenly
Those little sounds

Of toddler laughs and
Splashing water

The sounds of you —
My world, my daughter.

IN THE DARK

Turned out the light
Switched off my phone

Sat in the dark
You and I, alone.

Rocking we sat
Where we've sat since when

I first brought you home
You were so tiny then.

Back and forth
The rocking chair goes

The familiar beat
Your little self knows

As you curl against me
The warmth and the sway

Send you to slumber
In your favourite way

Of skin against skin
And milky goodnights

Of closeness and rocking
Alone, you and I.

Little, yes still
But bigger still yet

And I know it'll keep going —
So much bigger you'll get.

But now here in the dark
Just as before

You and I, alone
My baby once more.

I WANT YOU
TO KNOW

Darling, I'm so tired today
I'd love more time in bed

I'd love a little sleep in
To rest my weary head.

Daddy's made a fort for you
Maybe you can play?

Once I've had some rest, my love,
Then we'll start our day.

Pitter patter, pitter patter
Toddle to my side

Whisper to me "mama" as
Your arms stretch open wide.

Ok darling, yes, I'm here
Mummy's getting up

You take me by my finger
And hand me a teacup.

You smile with delight
And just like that I smile too

Seeing you so happy
To have me come with you.

Suddenly sleep is back of mind
I sit legs crossed and waiting

For a tiny teddy tea party
And our make-believe baking.

Although I'm very tired
And I'd really love some rest

When I see your little smile
In an instant I forget.

Your presence is like sunshine
And I just want you to know

You simply make me happy
My dear, I love you so.

BEFORE YOU
GROW A
LITTLE MORE

You hand me your toy, smiling
As you ask me, please, to play

Showing me the newest words
You've learnt throughout the day.

I pull you in and cradle you
Like so many times before

Except you're a little longer now
You've grown a little more.

I peer down at my elbows crook
Where your tiny feet once sat

And see those little feet now
Dangle further on than that.

I notice it, randomly
In the subtlest of ways

How quickly you are growing
How fast they go, these days.

I cradle you, and rock
And you laugh at me with glee

An 'in joke' now, of yours and mine
Though bittersweet to me.

I'm here with you, every day
I've never missed a thing

Yet it seems suddenly
I've blinked and now we're in

The time where I look back and say
"I remember when"

It only seems like yesterday
I slowly counted ten

Of your tiny fingers
And of your tiny toes

I marvelled at your blonde hair
And your tiny button nose.

Now you laugh and sing along
Take me by the hand

Playing games of make believe
As we frolic in the sand.

I feel as though I've missed it
Even though I've been right here

Cheering every win
And wiping every tear.

And I know it now, it's played its game
This cheeky thing called time

As I think of how you've grown
And how quickly it's flown by

And I find myself standing here
Nostalgic and aghast

Thinking of your infant days
And how they're in the past.

I rock you now, back and forth
Like so many times before

As I laugh along with you
Before you grow a little more.

ON THE RUN

Now listen here, child of mine
Where is it that you go?

One second, you're in the loungeroom
The next I do not know.

Your little feet have learned to run
It seems for me the time has come

To learn to grow some extra eyes
It's real now, I'm a mum.

Kitchen mess, laundry piles
Sweat drips down my brow

Waking up at sparrow's crow
Not resting til sundown.

Run run run, up and down
The hallway all day long

Suddenly it's quiet.
Something must be wrong.

Run and yell "where'd you go?"
Find you standing there

Little hands and guilty eyes
Paper everywhere.

My goodness how I laugh these days
At all the things you do

And then I stop in disbelief
At just how fast you grew.

Running, jumping, tea parties
Bubbles in the bath

Speaking new words every day
Telling jokes to make me laugh.

You're not but long a one year old
But this age might be my favourite

Exhausted yes, enamoured too
I do my best to savour it.

Yes, this might just be my favourite age
I think it might be true

But I suppose if you asked me next month
I'd say the same thing too!

Off you go, child of mine
Run with all your might

For even though you're growing fast
I'll hold you in the night

Kiss upon your little head
Whisper softly how

I'll love every moment of your life
And my favourite will always be "now".

SMILES

I love the little smiles
Of drivers passing by

As they see us picking flowers
Nostalgia in their eyes.

I love their little nods
That tell me with no words

How they have been here too
Finding rocks and watching birds.

The linger of their gaze
It tells me simply that

These days are just so short
That soon I will look back

And feel the softness of your skin
As you ran and took my hand

Walking slow for hours
With our shoes off in the sand.

Yes, I love the little smiles
Of drivers passing by

Because they make me realise
How time... it truly flies.

That soon it will be I
Who's sitting at that wheel

Gazing out with warmth
And remembering the feel

Of the softness of your little hand
Passing rocks to mine —

Those littlest of moments
The greatest of all time.

So I smile back and wave
Then turn and say to you

Look a car, wave hello!
You point and say "broom broom!"

Time stands still, I breathe it in
The sweetest sound of you

As you babble while the sun sets
By birds' melodic tune.

Through misty eyes and broken voice
I ask you "shall we go?

It's time to find some other rocks
Where are they? Do you know?"

And, your hand in mine, I think once more
Of that passer-by's smile

That said to me "I was once you
One day, you will be I".

IN WONDER

I take it in with wonder
Your hair and nose and eyes

Your happiness that fills
Your whole body when you smile.

I stare at you with wonder
As you dance and sing and play

Your babbles as you tell me
Of the things you've seen each day.

I listen now with wonder
To the sounds that you can make

The sentences you're forming
The pride in which you take.

I hold you as I wonder
When it was it came to be

My tiny newborn baby grew
To the toddler I now see.

I think of you in wonder
Amazed at all you are

The simple fact of 'you'
A concept still so hard

To understand, for it feels
Like only yesterday

I saw that second line that said
You were on the way.

They told me time would move fast
They told me hold on tight

They told me you would grow right
Before my very eyes.

It's just that you can't know what
Those words, they truly mean

Until you're in the moment
Unsure of where you've been?

I know that I have seen them
Each smile, every tear

But I feel that I just blinked
And now we're in your second year.

I've been here every moment
I'll be here still, each day

I'll breathe in every moment
While you take my breath away.

PLAYING ON YOUR OWN

I sit to watch you play
For a while on your own

I stay so very quiet
So that you do not know.

You line up all your animals
Give them a cup of tea

Turn around in wonder
At every toy you see.

I should be doing laundry
Or cleaning up the dishes

Instead, I stay in silence
As I see you blowing kisses

To your dollies as you wave goodbye
Off on a new adventure

Then change your mind and collect them
"We'll explore this world, together!"

Off you run, lion in hand
Doll under your arm

I think of how I've watched you
With love right from the start

When I saw you take your first breath
For the very first time

As you lay so soft upon me
And your eyes gazed into mine.

Now you turn and see me
Your toys, they drop at once

Your little feet they toddle
Beg me to join the fun

And here I sit as tears they form
Within my mother eye

I watch in pure amazement
Silent questions: how and why?

You're suddenly not a baby
But a person of your own.

At the time I didn't realize
But I'm learning as I go

That I thought I truly loved you
The most your day of birth

Not knowing I would love you
More each day you have on earth.

THIS BED

This bed of ours
The centre of

This story of
The journey of us.

The bed in which
My waters broke

In which we lay
Our first night home.

Where hours spent
Feeding you

Burping, rocking
Playing too.

Where bassinet was
By my side

Eventually
Though, cast aside.

This bed the place
Of home to you

Of mum and dad
Of comfort too

Of hours spent
Sitting up

Cradling you
Through the rough

Teething nights
And runny noses

And everything else
Life has thrown us.

As we've grown
So has it

This bed the place
Of game and wit

Of parachutes
And giggling

Of story time
And wriggling.

This bed the place
Where you now lay

Every night
And every day.

Darling so much
More to me

Than wood and foam
And white bed sheets.

This bed the home
Of memories —

The ones of us
Of you and me.

PUDDLES

Me and you, you and I
Adore our time together

You wake each day and say "outside"
Regardless of the weather.

Chomp chomp, brush brush
Ok, I say, get ready

Shoes are on, out the door
Clutching your pal teddy.

Splish splash, splish splash
Jumping with no care

Take your hand and run so fast
Leap into the air.

He he, ha ha
Turn and ask for more

Laughing hard, you and I
Until our cheeks are sore.

Up up, more more
Arms stretch up to me

Pick you up and swing you round
Play our make believe.

Quack quack, duck duck
We waddle to the water

Laugh and squeal with delight
In these moments with my daughter.

Quick kiss, long hug
Rain drops on your face

Run back home, dry clothes on
Warm in my embrace.

Pitter patter, pitter patter
Little feet, they go

To the door and gaze outside
I really hope you know

Heart warms, time slows
I sit and stare at you

You ask if we can play some more
There's nothing else I'd rather do.

RUSH THROUGH LIFE

Sometimes I rush through life and
I forget to smell the roses

Days go by so quickly
Changing nappies, wiping noses.

Today I tried to hurry
Rushing so that you

Wouldn't see me changing bed sheets —
Your favourite thing to do.

You like to lay down, eyes up high
As sheets fly overhead

The beauty that you see in
The simple making of a bed.

I rushed because I worried that
You'd see me and declare

"Up" with eyes wide open
And arms stretched in the air.

I worried that you'd want to play
Within those crisp white sheets

As I moved them softly up and down
While you laughed and kicked your feet.

I worried that this playing
Would slow the days flow down

As I'd rest the flying sheet and
You'd beg for another round.

Well, sweet one, you saw me.
You never miss a thing

And so I raised you up to
The bed and put you in.

Higher, higher, up they went!
The sheets flew here and there!

You waved and kicked your legs about
Your laughter filled the air.

It stopped right there, that clock of mine
And for moments time stood still

As I watched you live your life, just —
So present, and so joyful.

I threw the sheets up high again
And tears formed in my eyes

As I watched your face light up with glee
For its then I realized

How much I've really rushed it all
This truly lovely life

And what a wonderful thing you're giving me
The chance to see it through your eyes.

TWEET
TWEET

You don't know many words yet
But there's one you love for sure

"Outside"; you learned it early on
And you say it more and more.

I've never really been one
To venture in the wild

But then this is the beauty
Of growing with your child.

"Teet teet" you say, finger high
Pointing to the sky

Watching wings spread
With eyes in wonder, open wide.

We sit there then, you and I
By birds' euphonic song

...To think of all the things I've missed
Until you came along.

My child, you have given me
This second chance at life

To see the wonder in the things
That used to pass me by.

With you I see the beauty
In the simplest of things

Two butterflies in their dance
Leaves drifting in the wind.

I see it now, just like you
This world, in such deep focus

Awakened all my senses
To the magic all around us.

I study your sweet little eyes
In wonder as you see

How wonderful this life is
And then it dawns on me

As windswept hair falls in your eyes
Your smile pure and wide

How much it is you teach me
My heart, it fills with pride.

As tear drops fall upon my cheek
I take your hand and run

Feet moving bare upon the grass
We dance under the sun.

Round and round then down we go
Collapsed in bouts of laughter

Sharing in the wonder
Of this world of yours, my daughter.

THE LITTLE THINGS

I wonder if the little things
That make up every day

Are the things that I will think about
With tears in eye and say

"I miss your tiny shoes
And the patter of those feet

Running down the hallway
As you learn to pick up speed".

"I miss the messy chaos
Your toys strewn on the floor

As you carry many all at once
Unsure which you love more".

"I miss the time on hand and knee
Around you while you eat

As you conduct your arms left and right
Food scattering round your seat".

"I miss the way you toddle round
Head bowed and two feet flying

Rushing to get close to me
In laughter or when crying".

"I miss the nights of you with us
When in the dark I see

Your tiny hands reaching out
Stretched in search of me".

Darling, one day there'll be no mess
No little shoes lined at the door

Meals will all be eaten up
You won't sleep in our bed anymore.

It's bittersweet, the thought of this
Because of course that day

Will still be part of life with you
Where new memories will be made.

But never again will you be as small
As, my darling, you are now

Time keeps playing tricks on me
Where did it go, and how?

Although I wait with wonder
To see who you will be

I know I'll miss the little things
Of these days, just you and me.

LAUGHING IN YOUR SLEEP

Laughing in your sleep, my sweet
what is it that you dream of?

Watch you as your cheeks fly up
for that laugh of yours I so love.

Tell me, darling child
was it daddy's silly faces?

Was it mummy's tummy kisses
or us finding hidey spaces?

Peekaboo, where are you?
Books of words and numbers —

Of which of these do you dream
amidst your evening slumber?

Watching you, smiling too
makes my soul so light

That all we do, darling, with you
brings such joy in to your night.

WATCH YOU GROW

I look forward to meeting you.

I already know you, it's true, but the you that I know is the you that we now see —

I wonder, who is it that you will be?

I spend each day in surrender to the majestic unknown; along for the ride, floating with the tides of the ever changing you, eager and expectant, each day and always.

There is no pressure, no expectation, you do not owe me anything, now or ever. I merely allow myself this, a simple pleasure, through all of my devotion; the warm embrace of this enamoured anticipation.

Each day, sweet one, spent soaking you in as you are, and yet surrounded with an eagerness to learn the you of morrow; every growth of yours a growth of mine, showing me a love I never knew possible and expanding it, constantly, alongside you, for you, amazingly so.

I trace the lines of your golden hair in slumber, contemplating, imagining, the endless scenarios and versions of you. The clearest, truest and most constant component always, of course, that —

I adore you. Simply. Entirely. Unconditionally. In whatever, whoever, however you become.

So, my darling, I want you to know I look forward to it,

meeting you,

each and every day; my greatest excitement, my greatest joy.

And that I love you, all forms of you; now, then, when, endlessly.

ACKNOWLEDGEMENTS

Thank you to my husband, who has held my hand through so many of life's adventures, without your support and encouragement this book would never have come to be. Thank you for listening, planning, proofreading, and giving late night crash courses in Microsoft word. Most of all, thank you for being such an amazing daddy, and giving me the time I so needed to work on this book. When I see you with our daughter, everything makes sense.

Thank you to my own mother, who has led me with such grace through these early stages of motherhood, and has guided me, as always, to listen to and trust my own inner voice. You happily read every single poem or chapter as soon as it's finished, no matter day or night, and that means more to me than you could ever know.

Thank you to Bec, for your enthusiasm, kindness and editing excellence. Someone had to monitor my enthusiastic over-use of commas and semi-colons, and I was so happy when you responded immediately with "Would absolutely love to!" Grateful for you.

Thank you to my collective 'mum friends', both real life and online, who have surrounded me with acceptance and support, heard me when I needed to be heard, and helped me to listen to myself when I needed it the most.

And the biggest thank you, of course, to my sweet girl. I feel I have travelled lifetimes with you already, my greatest joy, my greatest inspiration, the greatest love I have ever known.

ABOUT THE AUTHOR

Jess lives in Australia with her husband and daughter.

She has always had a love for writing which, in her own words, 'up until now usually manifested in infrequent, but deeply invested, dabblings in creative speeches and long-winded birthday cards'.

It was always a dream of hers to write a book, and it wasn't until the birth of her daughter, and the beginning of her motherhood journey, that the words just began to flow.

From the Rocking Chair is her first book.

Find more from Jess online at 🅞 @fromtherockingchair.

Ingram Content Group UK Ltd.
Milton Keynes UK
UKHW020613200623
423737UK00013B/412

9 780645 330502